East Lynne
or Lady Isabel's Shame

EAST LYNNE

or Lady Isabel's Shame

a melodrama in three acts

by

BRIAN J. BURTON

based on the novel by Mrs Henry Wood

C. COMBRIDGE LTD
WRENTHAM STREET · BIRMINGHAM 5

First published 1965
by C. COMBRIDGE LTD.,
WRENTHAM STREET,
BIRMINGHAM 5
© Brian J. Burton 1964

PRINTED IN GREAT BRITAIN, BY DREW AND HOPWOOD LTD, BIRMINGHAM 3

INTRODUCTION

'East Lynne' by Mrs Henry Wood (born Ellen Price, the daughter of a Worcester glove manufacturer) was first published in 1861 in serial form. It aroused considerable interest during serialisation and when it was published in book form it was the subject of a most enthusiastic review in 'The 'Times' which was followed by similar criticalac claim from other reviewers. Since that day it has sold millions of copies, has been translated into many languages, and adapted for the stage.

The first version to be presented in dramatic form is reputed to be one by W. Archer which was staged at the Effingham Theatre in Whitechapel exactly a hundred years ago on November 12th 1864. This was followed, in February 1866, by a version presented at the Surrey Theatre which was revived in 1867 with Wilson Barrett in the cast. Since then, at least sixteen different versions have been licensed by the Lord Chamberlain's Office for public performance.

Very few of these adaptations were published and they remain only in manuscript form. Those that were published are T. A. Palmer's version in 1874, which was issued by Samuel French, and an anonymous adaptation in the 'Dick's Standard Play' series about 1883.

This new version, which I have sub-titled 'Lady Isabel's Shame', is not based on any previous play but has been adapted direct from the novel. Nevertheless, I have included one or two lines from the Victorian versions where they do not appear in the novel and yet have become an essential part of any dramatisation of 'East Lynne'. An example is the famous 'Dead, dead and never called me Mother' which was the invention of T. A. Palmer and not of Mrs Henry Wood. What play of 'East Lynne' would be complete without this immortal line?

The object of this adaptation has been to provide a version of the novel which can be performed in one set by a limited number of players and yet remains faithful to Mrs Henry Wood's novel with its main plot and several involved sub-plots. In order to do this, I have had to sacrifice a number of minor characters and although students of Mrs Henry Wood may regret the passing of 'Little Willie' from the cast list, I am certain that any theatrical producer about to tackle this play will breathe a sigh of relief.

BRIAN J. BURTON.
1964

To my mother

CHARACTERS IN THE PLAY

ARCHIBALD CARLYLE—*the master of East Lynne*

ISABEL CARLYLE—*his wife*

CORNELIA CARLYLE—*his unmarried sister*

LORD MOUNTSEVERN—*Isabel's only living relative*

BARBARA HARE—*secretly in love with Archibald*

RICHARD HARE—*her brother—a fugitive from justice*

FRANCIS LEVISON—*an unscrupulous rogue with designs on Isabel*

JOYCE HALLIJOHN—*an upper-maid at East Lynne*

WILSON—*a maidservant*

SYNOPSIS OF SCENES

The action of the play takes place in the sitting room of Archibald Carlyle's residence at East Lynne.

| ACT ONE: | *Scene One:* | June 1850—late evening |
| | *Scene Two:* | A month later |

| ACT TWO: | *Scene One:* | A few years later |
| | *Scene Two:* | Later the same evening |

ACT THREE:	*Scene One:*	Several years later
	Scene Two:	Eighteen months later
	Scene Three:	One month later

The running time of this play is approximately two hours (excluding intervals).

EAST LYNNE or LADY ISABEL'S SHAME was first presented by the Brotherhood Players at the Memorial Hall, Chingford on November 18th 1964, with the following cast:-

ARCHIBALD CARLYLE	Alan Lumley
ISABEL CARLYLE	Pat Rolfe
CORNELIA CARLYLE	Jean Ezra
LORD MOUNTSEVERN	Reginald Clark
BARBARA HARE	Ann Dempsey
RICHARD HARE	Robert Borrow
FRANCIS LEVISON	Peter McAndrew
JOYCE HALLIJOHN	Barbara Rogers
WILSON	Pat Taylor

The play was directed by ALFRED ROGERS
with setting and costumes designed by PETER McANDREW
and lighting by DAVID BINGHAM and DON HATCHER
Stage direction by RONALD BROWN
Photographs by SQUIRE, Chingford.

ACT ONE

SCENE ONE

The sitting room at East Lynne furnished in the style of the mid-nineteenth century.

There are double doors in the centre of the rear wall through which can be seen a hallway. To the left of the hall, but out of view of the audience, is the front door. To the right a corridor leading to a conservatory, the rest of the living rooms and the staircase to the upper rooms.

On the left-hand wall of the sitting room are french windows leading to the garden. On the right-hand wall is a fireplace with a door upstage of it which leads to the dining room and the servants' quarters.

An armchair stands below the fireplace and a sofa to the left of it. There is a table down left with one upright chair above it and another to the left of it. A piano and stool stand against the back wall to the left of the double doors and a long table on the right of them.

The walls are hung with oil paintings in ornate frames and the room is dressed with a great deal of fussy Victoriana.

When the curtain rises it is late evening on a Friday in June 1850.

CORNELIA CARLYLE, *a tall angular women in her late forties, is seated on the left end of the sofa with* JOYCE HALLIJOHN, *an upper servant in her middle twenties, standing to her right.*

Cornelia: Joyce, is everything prepared in Mr Carlyle's apartment?
Joyce: Yes, Miss Carlyle. We've made everything look as cheerful as possible.
Cornelia (*aside*): Cheerful indeed — and for her! (*Aloud*) Well there — do get along about your business, for I expect them here every minute now.
Joyce: Very good, Miss Carlyle. (*Exit right*).

9

Cornelia: I'm sure I'd as soon see Archibald Carlyle hanged as married. Haven't I, his own sister, been more like a mother to him? Didn't I love him more than anything else in the world? And what has been my reward? To be discarded with contemptuous indifference so that he might take a young wife to his bosom, to be loved more than I have been. I always thought that he loved that girl a great deal better than he should. At least I can be grateful for one thing — that silly Barbara Hare has not got him, after all the years she's been running after him. A woman has no business to chase after a man like that — it's not decent. Not that this Isabel Vane is much better with her high and mighty ideas. That is why I've decided to make East Lynne my home for the future. Here, I can watch over Archibald's interests for I know she'll bring him to beggary. Besides, I see no reason to keep up the expense of two establishments.

    Enter JOYCE *right*.

Joyce: Excuse me, ma'am. I can hear the carriage wheels on the drive. Mr Carlyle is here, ma'am, with his bride.
Cornelia: Well, go along, girl, and let them in. What are you waiting for?
Joyce: Yes, ma'am. (*Exit up left*).
Cornelia: Well, there's one thing I know for certain. I will never forgive him nor tolerate her.

    ARCHIBALD *and* ISABEL *enter up left. He is in his late twenties —
a handsome, gentle man.* ISABEL, *little more than a girl, is very
beautiful with fair hair and a pale complexion. They come to
centre stage,* ISABEL *on* ARCHIBALD's *left.* MISS CARLYLE *rises.*

Archibald (*crossing to* CORNELIA *in front of the sofa*): You here, Cornelia! That was kind. How are you? (*Turning to* ISABEL *and bringing her down*) Isabel, this is my sister.
Isabel: How do you do, Miss Carlyle?
Cornelia (*coldly*): I hope you are well, ma'am.
Archibald: If you will excuse me, there are some trifles I must collect from the carriage. I will leave you with my sister, Isabel. (*He goes out up left*).

Cornelia: No doubt you will wish to go upstairs and take off your things before supper, ma'am.

Isabel: Thank you, I will go to my rooms, but I do not require supper. We have dined. I will just rest here for a few moments. I am extremely tired after that exhausting journey. (*Sits left end of sofa.* CORNELIA *remains standing by fireplace*).

Cornelia: If you do not require supper, ma'am, what will you take?

Isabel: Some tea, if you please. I am very thirsty.

Cornelia: Tea! So late as this? I don't know that they have boiling water at this hour. Besides, you'd never sleep a wink all night if you took tea at eleven o'clock.

Isabel: Oh — then never mind. It is of no consequence. Do not let me give trouble.

Cornelia (*sniffing*): I hope you will be contented at East Lynne.

Isabel: Contented! Why of course I shall. The dear old place. I was very happy here when I was a child; and it was here that poor Papa died, too. And then Archibald came and bought the place, and he was very kind to me, also. I do believe it was that which first made me learn to love him.

Cornelia: Archibald has a very kind and generous nature.

Isabel: He has indeed, and I shall try to be a good wife to him, and render him as happy as possible. I have been thinking how I can be of service to him, and I mean to try and persuade him to let me ride to town with him every morning, and assist him with his legal affairs, and be his confidential clerk. Do you think he will let me?

Cornelia: He'd be a fool if he did. (*Snorts*).

   ISABEL *bursts into tears.* ARCHIBALD *enters up left.*

Archibald (*coming down to* ISABEL'S *left and putting his arm round her shoulders*): Isabel! My darling, what ails you?

Isabel: I am tired and coming into this house again made me think of Papa. I should like to go to my rooms, Archibald, but I do not know which they are.

Cornelia: The best rooms; those next to the library. Shall I go with you, my lady?

Isabel: Thank you, but I know my way. (*Moves up centre and turns at door*) Archibald!

Archibald (*going up to her*): What is it, my love?

Isabel: I do feel tired, Archibald, very tired and low-spirited. May I undress at once and not come down here again tonight?

Archibald: May you not come down again? Have you forgotten that you are, at last, in your own home? A happy home, I trust, it will be to you, my darling. I will strive to render it so. By all means retire at once, but will you not take something before you do so? Some tea, perhaps?

Isabel: No thank you.

Archibald: But you must take something. You complained of thirst in the carriage.

Isabel (*with a glance across at* CORNELIA): Water will do — will be best for me, I mean. My maid, Marvel, can get it for me. (*Exit up right*).

Archibald (*coming down to* CORNELIA *who has seated herself on the sofa right during* ISABEL'S *last speech*): Cornelia, I do not understand all this. I have not seen one of the servants whom I engaged, but I see yours. Where are mine?

Cornelia (*off-hand*): Gone away.

Archibald: Gone away! What for? I believe they were excellent servants.

Cornelia: Very excellent. Decking themselves out in their finery on a Saturday morning. Archibald, never attempt to dabble in domestic affairs again for you only get taken in.

Archibald: But what did they do wrong?

Cornelia: Enough of the servants. I have other matters to discuss with you — important matters. Archibald Carlyle, how could you go and make a fool of yourself? If you must have married, were there not plenty of young ladies in your own sphere of society —

Archibald: Stay! I wrote you a full statement of my motives and actions, Cornelia. I concealed nothing that it was necessary you should know. I am not disposed to enter upon further discussion of the subject, and you must pardon my saying so. Let us return to the topic of the servants. Where are they?

Cornelia: I sent them away because they were superfluous encumbrances. We have four in the house, and I have no doubt that my lady has brought a fine maid — which makes five.

Archibald: No, Cornelia, they are your servants.

Cornelia: Exactly. I have come to live here.

Archibald: To live here! And what about your own home?

Cornelia: I have let it furnished. The people entered today. You cannot turn me out of East Lynne into the road, or to furnished lodgings, Archibald. There will be enough expense without our keeping on two houses; and most people, in your place, would jump at the prospect of my living here. Your wife will be mistress; I do not intend to take her honours from her; but I shall save her a world of trouble in management, and be useful to her as a housekeeper. She will be glad of that, inexperienced as she is. I dare say she never gave a domestic order in her life.

Archibald: There is certainly room for you at East Lynne, Cornelia, but —

Cornelia: A little too much. I think a house half its size might content us all, and still be grand enough for Lady Isabel.

Archibald (*moving away left*): East Lynne is mine, Cornelia.

Cornelia: So is your folly!

Archibald (*turning to* CORNELIA): And with regard to servants, I shall certainly keep as many as I think necessary. I cannot give my wife splendour, but I will give her comfort. The horses and carriages will take one man's time to —

Cornelia: What on earth are you talking about?

Archibald: I bought a pretty open carriage in town and a pair of ponies for it.

Cornelia (*rising*): Oh, Archibald! The sins that you are committing!

Archibald: Sins?

Cornelia (*moving to centre stage*): Wilful waste makes woeful want.

Archibald: Never fear, Cornelia, that I shall run beyond my income. But let us talk of this no further. I will mix some wine and water for Isabel. (*Moving up to long table right*) Shall I mix some for you?

Cornelia: I will mix some for myself should I require any. And now, I think, I will retire. (*Moving up to double doors and turning to* ARCHIBALD) And remember, Archibald, that which I taught you as a child. To be thrifty is a virtue; to squander is a sin. Goodnight, Archibald. (*Exit up right*).

Archibald: Goodnight, Cornelia. (*Aside*) Now am I married to my dear Isabel. How I intend to cherish this fair flower I have won. Although I know that she does not find it in her heart to love me as I love her, my earnest hope, day and night, is that one day she may learn to do so.

Enter ISABEL *up right in her dressing gown.*

Isabel (*going to* ARCHIBALD *up right centre*): Oh, Archibald, Archibald!

Archibald (*putting down the glass and holding* ISABEL): Isabel, what is the matter?

Isabel (*grasping him*): I grew nervous after Marvel went. I could not find the bell and that made me worse; so I came downstairs to find you. Why have you not come up yet?

Archibald: I have been talking to Cornelia. She wishes to remain with us here at East Lynne. I do not know what to decide. On one hand, I think she might save you the worry of household management; on the other I fancy we will be happier by ourselves.

Isabel (*her heart sinking*): As you and Miss Carlyle please, Archibald.

Archibald (*earnestly*): I wish it to be as you please. That is, I wish matters to be arranged as may best please you; and I will have them so arranged. My chief object in life now is your happiness.

Isabel: Let her stay, Archibald. She will not incommode us.

Archibald: At any rate, it can be tried for a month or two and we shall see how it works. But I was forgetting that you have been frightened. Come sit here beside me and tell me what it was that alarmed you. (*Leads her to sofa. They sit,* ISABEL *right,* ARCHIBALD *left*) Now, what made you nervous?

Isabel: Oh, I was very foolish. I kept thinking of frightful things. They would come into my mind. Do not blame me, Archibald. The bedroom is the same one in which Papa died.

Archibald (*with deep feeling*): Blame you, my darling!

Isabel: I thought of a dreadful story about the bats that the servants told. It was the night before Papa died. One of the servants mentioned that the bats had been round the house all evening. We looked out of the window and there they were — flying about in scores, in hundreds, a cloud of them diving at the window and flapping their wings. Right inside they came and would have touched our faces, only we drew back. Mrs Mason asked Wills, the servant, what it meant. She said she had never seen them so thick or so near. Then Mrs Mason asked her again what it was the sign of and she told us that it was a sure sign that death was at the very door of the house. I turned to the window again and — and — and —

Archibald: What was it you saw?

Isabel: Nothing — nothing at all. There was not a single bat to be seen. They had all gone, disappeared in that little space of time. I kept thinking about that tonight and I had the sudden fear that they might be at the windows now, behind the blinds. And then I was afraid to look at the bed. I fancied I might see —

Archibald (*rising and moving up to long table*): Come, my dear, I have mixed some wine and water for you. I was about to bring it up to you. (*Giving her the glass and remaining upstage of the sofa*) Your rooms shall be changed tomorrow, Isabel.

Isabel (*drinking wine*): No, let us remain in those. I shall like to feel that Papa was once their occupant. I won't grow nervous again.

Archibald (*picking up the lamp from the long table*): Come then. (*Holds out his hand to her*).

 ISABEL *moves up to him and they exit up right with the lamp.*

CURTAIN

ACT ONE
SCENE TWO

A MONTH LATER. WILSON, *a maidservant in her early twenties, is dusting left.* JOYCE *enters right.*

Wilson: Oh, Joyce, have you heard who is to come here today? The Hares and she among them. I heard Miss Cornelia telling Cook.

Enter ISABEL *up centre. She remains at the door unseen by* WILSON *and* JOYCE.

Joyce: Who is coming here — what are you chattering about?

Wilson: Why, Miss Barbara Hare to be sure. Only fancy her coming to pay a wedding visit here! My lady had better take care that she don't get a bowl of poison mixed for her. Master's out, or else I'd have given a shilling to see the interview between the three of them.

Joyce: Wilson, you had better take care what you say here. Go and see if there is anything you can do to assist with the preparations, if we are to have company.

Wilson: Oh, very well, but you mark my words, there'll be trouble there before very many more days are out. (*Exit right*).

JOYCE *starts to move up to the double doors as* ISABEL *enters as though she had just come into the room.*

Joyce: My lady!

Isabel: Ah, there you are, Joyce. I have been looking for you. There is a matter I wish to discuss with you.

Joyce: With me, my lady?

Isabel: Yes. (*Moves to table left and sits in upstage chair*) Come here, Joyce. (JOYCE *moves to right of table*) As you know, my maid Marvel has given notice and left my employ. How would you like the situation of lady's maid? That is if Miss Carlyle will agree to the transfer.

Joyce (*her face lighting up with pleasure*): Oh, my lady, you are very kind. I should so like it. I would serve you faithfully to the best of my ability; and I know I could do your hair well, if you allowed me to try. I have been practising on my own, night and morning.

"*If this be true, I care not who shall be the instrument of my revenge*"

ISABEL *and* FRANCIS LEVISON

Act II Scene I

"And what could possibly excite you, Wilson?"
CORNELIA, WILSON *and* JOYCE   *Act III Scene III*

"But who would believe my stor
ARCHIBALD *and* RICHARD   *Act II*

Isabel: But Miss Carlyle may not be inclined to transfer you to me.

Joyce: I think she would, my lady. She said, a day or two ago, that I appeared to suit you, and that you might have me altogether if you wished.

Isabel (*rising*): Very well then — all is settled.

Joyce: But there is one thing, my lady.

Isabel: Well, what is it?

Joyce: I scarce know how to aquaint you with the facts, my lady.

Isabel: Facts? I think you had better tell me all about it, Joyce. (*Sits in same chair*) Come sit here, at the table and you shall tell me what is troubling you.

Joyce (*incredulously*): Sit down, my lady?

Isabel: Certainly. Come.

JOYCE *crosses in front of the table and sits left of it.*

Joyce: I'll tell you as shortly as I can, my lady. I fear they are unpleasant facts.

Isabel: Go on, Joyce.

Joyce: My father was a clerk in Mr Carlyle's office — of course I mean the late Mr Carlyle. My mother died when I was eight years old, and my father afterwards married again — a governess she was. At the end of a year Afy was born.

Isabel: Who?

Joyce: My half sister, Afy. In less than another year her mother died and an aunt sent for the child. I remained at home with my father. We lived in the prettiest cottage, my lady. It was in the wood and it was my father's own. Then, after a few years Afy's aunt died and she came home. She quite frightened us. Her notions of dress were fine — she was gay and giddy. My father didn't like it; we were only plain working people, and she wanted to set up for a lady. The next thing was she got aquainted with young Richard Hare.

Isabel: With whom did you say?

Joyce: Mr Justice Hare's only son, own brother to Miss Barbara. Afy was very flighty; she encouraged Mr Richard and he soon grew to love her, but he was rather simple and she used to laugh at him behind his back.

Isabel: Go on.

Joyce: She encouraged others too, and would have them there in the evening when the house was free.

Isabel: She had many admirers?

Joyce: The chief one, my lady, was Richard Hare. She became aquainted with somebody else, a stranger, who used to ride over from a distance to see her; but I fancy there was nothing in it; Mr Richard was the one. And it went on and went on till — till — he killed our father.

Isabel: Who killed your father?

Joyce: Richard Hare, my lady. One night my father told Afy, before me, that she must not see Mr Richard again. For when gentlemen go in secret after poor girls, it is well known they have not marriage in their thoughts. The next night Richard Hare shot my father.

Isabel: How very dreadful. What was done to Richard Hare?

Joyce: He escaped, my lady. He went off that night, and has never been heard of since. There's a judgement of murder out against him, and his own father would be the first to deliver him up to justice. It is a dreadful thing to have befallen the Hare family. It is killing Mrs Hare by inches. Afy —

Isabel: What is that name, Joyce?

Joyce: She was christened Aphrodite, my lady, but my father never called her anything but Afy. But I have not told you the worst yet. As soon as the inquest was over she went off after Richard Hare.

Isabel: Did she really do so?

Joyce: She did indeed, my lady. Nothing has been heard of either of them; and it is most likely that they went out of England — perhaps to Australia, perhaps to America; nobody knows. What with the shame of that, and the shock of my poor father's murder, I had an attack of illness. It was a nervous fever, and it lasted for a long time. Miss Carlyle had me at her house, and she and her servants nursed me through it. She is good at heart, my lady, is Miss Carlyle, only her manners are against her, and she will think herself better than other people. After that illness, I stayed with her as upper maid, and never went out to work again.

Isabel: How long is it since this happened?

Joyce: It will be four years next September, my lady. (*Rising*) And that was what I had to tell you, my lady, before you decide to take me into your service. It is not every lady would like to engage one whose sister has turned out so badly.

Isabel: I do not see that it should make any difference.

Joyce: Thank you, my lady, you are very kind. May I go now, my lady?

Isabel (*rising*): One thing further, Joyce. As I was coming into the room earlier I happened, by chance, to overhear part of your conversation with Wilson. What was it she said about Miss Hare giving me a bowl of poison? You should tell Wilson not to whisper so loudly.

Joyce: It was only a bit of nonsense, of course, my lady. The fact is, that people think Miss Barbara was much attached to Mr Carlyle, reguarly in love with him, and many thought it would be a match. But I don't fancy she would have been the one to have made him happy, with all her love.

Isabel (*moving away right*): Very well, Joyce. You may go.

Joyce: Yes, my lady, and thank you very much. (*Exit right*).

Isabel: So Archibald was the object of Barbara Hare's affection! Perhaps he too has loved her, perhaps he loves her still, and only married me out of sympathy. Oh, if I thought that it would drive me frantic. But, no—no—no! I will not harbour a thought as foolish as that. Mr Carlyle is an honourable man; he loves me truly — has he not told me so? He would never deceive me.

Enter CORNELIA *up right. She comes to centre stage.*

Cornelia: Lady Isabel, they are waiting for an order for dinner.

Isabel: An order for dinner. (*Aside*) What shall I say? I have never ordered a dinner in all my life. I must say something. (*Aloud*) A — something to roast and boil, if you please.

Cornelia: Something to roast and boil! Are you aware, Lady Isabel that an order such as that would only puzzle the butcher? He would be uncertain whether you desired a few pounds of meat or a whole cow!

Isabel: A whole cow? Bless me, Miss Cornelia, we would never eat a whole cow. (*Aside*) I have evidently made a mistake this time. I'll try again. (*Aloud*) Well then, Miss Cornelia, order as much meat as you think Archibald and yourself will require. I do not want any.

Cornelia: Shall I give the necessary orders for today? The fishmonger will be up presently.

Isabel (*relieved*): Oh, I wish you would. I have not been accustomed to it, but I must learn. I don't think I know anything about housekeeping.

Cornelia: I don't think you do. (*Aside*) Poor Archibald — so much for marrying against my will. (*Exit up right*).

Isabel (*moving to window and looking out*): How I wish Archibald would come. The time hangs heavily when he is from my side.

Enter JOYCE *up right*.

Joyce: My lady!

Isabel (*turning*): Yes, Joyce?

Joyce: It is Lord Mountsevern, my lady. He has just arrived and wants to see the master. I have told him Mr Carlyle will be home any time now and he wishes to speak to your ladyship.

Isabel: Then show his lordship in here at once, Joyce.

Joyce: Very good, my lady. (*Exit up right*).

Isabel: Lord Mountsevern here! What can he want that is so important that he should call without informing us in advance? Still, he is my only living relative and I am delighted that he has decided to visit us. (*Moves down left*).

JOYCE *enters up right*.

Joyce: Lord Mountsevern, my lady.

LORD MOUNTSEVERN *enters up right*. *Exit* JOYCE *closing doors*.

Lord M (*moving down left to right of* ISABEL): What is the meaning of this, Isabel? You are married!

Isabel: Yes, four weeks ago.

Lord M: And to Mr Carlyle, the lawyer. How did it come about?

Isabel: He asked me and I accepted him. He came to Castle Marling at Easter, and asked me then. I was very much surprised.

Lord M: Why was I kept in ignorance of this, Isabel?

Isabel: I did not know you were kept in ignorance of it. Mr Carlyle wrote to you, as did Lady Mountsevern.

Lord M: I suppose this comes of your father's having allowed the gentleman to dance daily attendance at East Lynne. And so you fell in love with him.

Isabel (*amused*): Indeed, no, I never thought of such a thing as falling in love with Mr Carlyle.

Lord M (*quickly*): Then don't you love him?

Isabel (*turning away — timidly*): No — no I don't love him and that is the truth. (*Turning back to* LORD MOUNTSEVERN) But I like him much — oh, very much. And he is good to me!

Lord M (*stroking his chin*): If you do not love Mr Carlyle, how comes it that you are so wise in the distinction between 'liking' and 'loving'? It cannot be that you love anyone else?

Isabel (*embarrassed*): I shall love my husband in time.

Lord M: My poor child! (*Sharply*) Who has been staying at Castle Marling since I left?

Isabel: Mrs Levison came down.

Lord M: I alluded to gentlemen — young men.

Isabel: Only Francis Levison.

Lord M: Francis Levison! You have never been so foolish as to fall in love with *him*.

ISABEL *is confused. She turns away from* LORD MOUNTSEVERN.

Lord M (*gravely*): Isabel, Captain Levison is not a good man. If ever you were inclined to think him one, dispossess your mind of the idea, and hold him at arm's distance. Drop his aquaintance; encourage no intimacy with him.

Isabel: I have already dropped it and I shall not take it up again. (*Turning to* LORD MOUNTSEVERN) But Lady Mountsevern must think well of him, or she would not have him there.

Lord M (*significantly*): She thinks none too well of him; none can do so of Francis Levison. He is her cousin, and is one of those idle, vain, empty-headed flatterers whom it is her pleasure to group about her. Do you be wiser, Isabel. But this does not solve the enigma of your marriage with Carlyle; on the contrary, it renders it the more unaccountable. He must have cajoled you into it.

Isabel: I can assure you that —

The double doors open and ARCHIBALD *enters. He comes down to right of* LORD MOUNTSEVERN *and offers his hand.*

Archibald: Lord Mountsevern, this is a most unexpected pleasure.

Lord M (*refusing* ARCHIBALD'S *hand and turning to* ISABEL): Isabel, I am sorry to turn you out of the room, but I wish to say a few words to Mr Carlyle.

Isabel: Certainly, sir. I'll retire to the garden at once. (*Exit through french window*).

Lord M: Now, sir, how came this marriage about? Do you possess so little honour, that, taking advantage of my absence, you must intrude yourself into my family and clandestinely espouse my ward, Lady Isabel Vane?

Archibald: My lord, I do not understand you.

Lord M: Yet I speak plainly. What is it but a clandestine procedure, to take advantage of a guardian's absence and beguile a young girl into a marriage beneath her?

Archibald: There has been nothing clandestine in my conduct towards Lady Isabel Vane; there shall be nothing but honour in my conduct towards Lady Isabel Carlyle. Your lordship has been misinformed.

Lord M: I have not been informed at all. I was allowed to learn this from the public papers; I, the only living relative of Lady Isabel.

Archibald: When I proposed for Lady Isabel —

Lord M (*sarcastically*): Less than two months ago.

Archibald (*calmly*): Less than two months ago, my first action, after Isabel accepted me, was to write to you. But that I imagine you may not have received the letter, by stating you first heard of our marriage through the papers, I should say the want of courtesy lay on your lordship's side for having vouchsafed me no reply to it.

Lord M: What were the contents of the letter?

Archibald: I stated what had occurred, mentioning what I was able to do in the way of settlements, also that both Isabel and myself wished that the ceremony might take place as soon as possible.

Lord M: And pray where did you address the letter?

Archibald: Lady Mountsevern could not give the address. She said, if I would entrust the letter to her she would forward it, for she expected daily to hear from you. I did give her the letter, and I heard no more of the matter, except that her ladyship sent me a message, when Isabel was writing to me, that as you had returned no reply, you, of course, approved.

Lord M (*moving away right to in front of the sofa*): I see — is this fact?

Archibald (*coldly*): My lord! Whatever may be my defects in your eyes, I am at least a man of truth. Until this moment, the suspicion that you were in ignorance of the contemplated marriage never occurred to me.

Lord M (*sitting on sofa*): So far, then, I beg your pardon, Mr Carlyle. But how came the marriage about at all? How came it to be hurried over in this unseemly fashion? You made the offer at Easter, Isabel tells me, and you married her three weeks after it.

Archibald (*moving to* LORD MOUNTSEVERN): And I would have married her and brought her away the day I did make it, had it been practicable. I have acted throughout for her comfort and happiness.

Lord M (*disagreeably*): Oh, indeed! Perhaps you will put me in possession of the facts, and of your motives.

Archibald: I warn you that the facts, to you, will not bear a pleasant sound, Lord Mountsevern.

Lord M: Allow me to be the judge of that.

Archibald: Business took me to Castle Marling on Good Friday. On the following day I called at your house; after your own and Isabel's invitation, it was natural that I should call; in fact it would have been a breech of good feeling not to do so. I found Isabel ill-treated and miserable, far from enjoying a happy home in your house —

Lord M (*rising*): What, sir? Ill-treated and miserable!

Archibald (*facing* LORD MOUNTSEVERN): Ill-treated even to blows, my lord. I learnt it, I must premise, through the chattering revelations of your little son. Isabel, of course, would not have mentioned it to me; but when the child had spoken she did not deny it. In short, she was too broken-hearted, too completely bowed in spirit, to deny it. It aroused all my feelings of indignation; it excited in me an irresistible desire to emancipate her from this cruel life, and take her where she could find affection and — I hope — happiness. There was only one way in which I could do this, and I risked it. I asked her to become my wife, and to return to her home at East Lynne.

Lord M: Then — am I to understand that, when you called that day at my house, you carried no intention with you of proposing to Isabel?

Archibald: Not any. It was a sudden step, called forth by the circumstances under which I found her.

Lord M (*abruptly*): May I enquire if you love her?

Archibald (*after a pause*): These are feelings man rarely acknowledges to man, Lord Mountsevern, but I will answer you. I do love her passionately and sincerely. I learnt to love her at East Lynne, but I could have carried my love silently within me to the end of my life, and never betrayed it, but for that unexpected visit to Castle Marling. If the idea of making her my wife had not previously occurred to me as practicable, it was that I deemed her rank incompatible with mine.

Lord M: As it was.

Archibald: Country solicitors have married peer's daughters before now. I only add another to the list.

Lord M: But you cannot keep her as a peer's daughter, I presume.

Archibald (*moving centre stage*): East Lynne will be her home. Our establishment will be small and quiet, as compared with her father's. I explained all this to Isabel at the first, and she might have retracted had she wished. East Lynne will descend to our eldest son, should we have children. My profession is most lucrative, my income good. Were I to die tomorrow, Isabel would enjoy East Lynne and about three thousand a year. I gave these details in the letter which appears to have miscarried. (*Pauses*) Your lordship perceives,

I hope, that there has been nothing 'clandestine' in my conduct to Lady Isabel.

Lord M (*crossing to* ARCHIBALD *and holding out his hand*): I refused your hand when I came in, Mr Carlyle, as you may have observed. Perhaps you will refuse yours now, though I should be proud to shake it. When I find myself in the wrong, I am not above acknowledging the fact, and I must state my opinion that you have behaved most kindly and honourably.

They shake hands.

Lord M (*in a whisper*): Of course, I cannot be ignorant that, in speaking of Isabel's ill-treatment, you alluded to my wife. Has it transpired beyond yourselves?

Archibald: You may be sure that neither Isabel nor myself would mention it. We shall dismiss it from amongst our reminiscences. Let it be as though you never heard it. It is past and done with.

Enter ISABEL *from the garden.*

Lord M: Isabel, I came here, this morning almost prepared to strike your husband and I go away honouring him. Be a good and faithful wife to him, for he deserves it.

Isabel (*surprised*): Of course I shall be.

Lord M: And now, with your permission, I'll take a look about the gardens.

Isabel: Most certainly. We will accompany you. (*They exit through the french window*).

After a moment CORNELIA *enters up left followed by* BARBARA HARE. *She is a very pretty girl of 23, self-assured and poised.* CORNELIA *leads the way to the sofa where they sit,* CORNELIA *on* BARBARA'S *right.*

Barbara: Papa was called away on business suddenly and Mama was not feeling too well, so I have ventured here alone.

Cornelia: I am glad you have come. I thought perhaps you would not be pleased with Archibald's selection of a wife.

Barbara: Not pleased, Miss Carlyle? Why, what have I to do with the choice of a wife?

Cornelia: Oh, nothing; only there are so many ladies in East and West Lynne that seemed to take such an interest in Archibald's welfare that I thought they might be disappointed in his marriage — that's all.

Barbara: On the contrary, I wish him all the happiness possible. He has ever treated me most kindly, and I sincerely hope he has found a wife worthy of him. Do you like her?

Cornelia: Better than I thought I should. I had expected airs and graces and pretence and I must say she is free from them. She seems quite wrapped up in Archibald and watches for his coming home as a cat watches for a mouse. She is dull without him.

Barbara: Dull! How does she employ her time?

Cornelia (*snappishly*): In doing nothing. Sings a bit, and reads a bit, and receives her visitors, and idles away her days in that manner. She coaxes Archibald out into the grounds after breakfast and he ought not to let himself be coaxed; it makes him late at the office. And then she dances down to the park gates with him, hindering him still further, for he would go alone in half the time. And in the evening she goes to meet him again. Oh, she is first with him now; business is second.

Barbara: (*feigning indifference*): I suppose it is natural.

Cornelia: I suppose it is absurd. I give them very little of my company, especially of an evening. They go strolling out together, or she sings to him, he is hanging over her as if she was gold. I'll tell you what I saw last night. Archibald had what he is not often subject to — a severe headache and he came into here after dinner and lay on this sofa. She carried a cup of tea to him, and never came back leaving her own on the table till it was perfectly cold. I pushed open the door to tell her so. There was my lady's cambric handkerchief, soaked in eau-de-cologne, lying on his forehead, and there was my lady herself kneeling down and looking at him, he with his arm thrown round her to hold her there. Now I ask you, Barbara, whether there's any sense in fadding with a man like that. If ever he had a headache before he was married, I used to mix him up a good dose of salts and senna, and tell him to go to bed and sleep the pain off.

Enter WILSON *from french window. She comes to centre stage.*

Wilson: Begging your pardon, ma'am.

Cornelia: What is it, Wilson?

Wilson: It's Blair, the gardener, ma'am — he says that the master has ordered him to make the geranium bed oval and that you said it was to be square, ma'am.

Cornelia: Oval indeed! He's a regular muff is that Blair, and as obstinate as a mule.

Wilson: He said that her ladyship preferred it to be oval.

Cornelia: Did he now. (*Rising*) I'll go and have a word with him at once. Excuse me, Miss Hare; it won't take me but a minute to settle this matter once and for all. (*Exit through french window with* WILSON).

Barbara (*rising and moving left centre*): And she is happy with him — the only man I ever loved. Why did he pass me by for a baby-faced girl like that? It cannot be that she is capable of loving him with the deep affection I might have bestowed on him. (*Sits in chair above table, sobbing*).

Enter ARCHIBALD *from french window. He sees* BARBARA *and comes to her right.*

Archibald: Barbara, are you ill? What is it? (*She cries hysterically*) Barbara, what can have caused all this?

Barbara (*turning to face him*): What can have caused it? *You* can ask me that?

Archibald: I don't understand you, Barbara. If I have offended you in any way, I am truly sorry.

Barbara: Truly sorry, no doubt! What do you care for me? If I go under the sod tomorrow, you have your wife to care for; what am I?

Archibald (*glancing at the window*): Hush!

Barbara: Hush, yes! What is my misery to you? I would rather be in my grave, Archibald Carlyle, than endure the life I lead. My pain is greater than I know how to bear.

Archibald (*moving away right*): I cannot affect to misunderstand you. (*Turning*) But, my dear Barbara, I never gave you cause to think that I — that I — cared for you more than I did.

Barbara (*rising*): Never gave me cause! When you have been coming to our house constantly, almost as my shadow; when you gave me this. (*Holding up a locket*) When you have been more intimate with me than a brother!

Archibald: Stay, Barbara. There it is — a brother. I have been nothing else. It never occurred to me to be anything else.

Barbara (*moving to him — almost losing control*): Ay — as a brother, nothing else! What cared you for my feelings? What recked you that you gained my love?

Archibald: Barbara, hush! Do be calm and reasonable. If ever I gave you cause to think I regarded you with deeper feeling, I can only express to you my deep regret, and assure you it was done unconsciously.

Barbara (*lifting her face to him*): If she had not come between us, should you have loved me?

Archibald: I don't know. How can I know? Do I not say to you, Barbara, that I only thought of you as a friend, as a sister? I cannot tell what might have been.

Barbara: I could bear it better but that it was known. All West Lynne has coupled us together in their prying gossip, and they have only pity to cast to me now. I would far rather you had killed me, Archibald.

Archibald: I can only express to you my deep regret. I can only hope you will soon forget it all. Let the remembrance of this conversation pass away this very day; let us still be to each other as friends — as brother and sister. Believe me, the confession has not lessened you in my estimation.

WILSON *appears at the window and watches the following scene.*

Archibald (*taking* BARBARA'S *hands in his*): God bless you, Barbara.

Barbara: I think I must have been mad to say what I did. Forget that it was uttered.

Archibald: I told you I would do so.

Barbara: You will not betray me to — your wife?

Archibald: Barbara!

Barbara: Thank you, Archibald.

Archibald (*still holding her hands*): In a short time, Barbara, I trust you will find one more worthy to receive your love than I have been.

Barbara (*impulsively*): Never. I do not love and forget so lightly. (*Moving up to door right and turning back to him*) In years to come, in my old age, I shall still be nothing but Barbara Hare. (*Exit right*).

WILSON *exits through french window.*

Archibald: I heartily pray that she will soon find someone to her liking and forget me. (*Sits on sofa*).

ISABEL *enters from the window. She crosses to* ARCHIBALD *who rises. They sit together on the sofa.* ARCHIBALD *on the left.*

Archibald: You are fatigued are you not?

Isabel: Oh, no, not in the least! Where is Barbara?

Archibald: She has withdrawn but a minute since. I think she may be in the conservatory.

Isabel: You say you have been intimate with the Hare family for a long time?

Archibald: Quite so. Cornelia is related to them.

Isabel: Do you think Barbara pretty?

Archibald: Very.

Isabel: Then — intimate as you were — I wonder you never fell in love with her — did you, Archibald?

Archibald: Did I what, Isabel?

Isabel: You never loved Barbara Hare?

Archibald: Loved her! What is your head running on, Isabel? I never loved but one woman; and that one I made my wife.

Isabel: I believe you, my dear husband.

Archibald: Enough of this foolish talk. (*Rising*) Come now you shall sing for me, and I will pay you with a kiss. (*Leads her to the piano where she sits to play. He stands on the right of the piano to turn the music*).

Isabel: What shall it be?

29

Archibald: You know — my favourite song.
Isabel: Alas — that was Papa's favourite too.
She sings 'The years that pass away'. (Words and music on pages 76-79)
Isabel: Why do you like the song so much, Archibald?
Archibald: I don't know. I never liked it so much until I heard it from you.
Isabel: I wonder if the guests have come in? Shall we go into the next room?
Archibald: Just one more verse and then will I pay you for the song.
She repeats the final verse during which time BARBARA *enters from right and stands watching them. At the end of the song* ARCHIBALD *bends over* ISABEL *and kisses her.* BARBARA *turns away distressed as*

THE CURTAIN FALLS

ACT TWO
SCENE ONE

A FEW YEARS LATER. ARCHIBALD *is standing left centre talking to* CAPTAIN FRANCIS LEVISON *who is on his right.* LEVISON *is a tall, handsome man of thirty with a polished, suave manner.*

Levison: 'Pon my soul, Carlyle, this game of hide and seek is infernally boring. I'm sick of Boulogne and all other places of refuge for the impecunious.

Archibald: Shall I see your uncle, Sir Peter, for you?

Levison: Will you?

Archibald: If you like. As your friend, you understand, not as your solicitor; that I should decline. I have a slight knowledge of Sir Peter. My father was well aquainted with him and, if I can render you any little service, I shall be happy to do so.

Levison: Really now, that is very kind of you.

Archibald: Not at all. What is more you may stay here at East Lynne until I can see your uncle and arrange with him about your affairs. I may prevail on him to relieve you once more from your embarrassments and make you a free man again.

Levison: How can I thank you enough, my dear fellow. I dread going abroad, away from all my friends, but I dread the bailiffs still more.

Archibald: You will be safe enough here. No one will think of looking for you in my house. So keep close and don't show yourself beyond the grounds. I will go, this very instant, and arrange for your rooms to be made ready. If you will excuse me.

LEVISON *bows to* ARCHIBALD *who exits right.*

Levison (*coming down centre*): So — I have been invited to stay at East Lynne! At last have I arranged the course of events so that I can be under the same roof as the fair Isabel. And now, if I play my cards cunningly she will soon be mine. Ah, someone is coming. I believe 'tis she! (*He moves to the window and looks out*).

ISABEL *enters up right, starts to move down centre and checks centre stage when she sees* LEVISON.

Isabel: Captain Levison — you here!

Levison (*turning from the window*): Indeed yes, Lady Isabel. Your husband has been so kind as to agree to assist me in straightening out a little matter of financial embarrassment. He has invited me to stay for a few days.

Isabel: To stay here! That cannot be. (*Moving down right*) That must not be!

Levison (*crossing to* ISABEL): Lady Isabel, we have both behaved like simpletons. If ever two beings were made to love each other, you and I were. I sometimes thought you read my feelings.

Isabel (*turning on him*): Francis Levison, sir!

Levison: I must speak, Lady Isabel, but a few words and then am I silent for ever. I would have declared myself years ago, but my debts, my uncertain position, my inability to keep a wife as your taste and style demanded, crushed my hopes, and so I suffered you to escape me.

Isabel: I will not listen to this language, sir!

Levison: One single moment yet, I pray you. I have long wished you to know why I lost you — a loss than tells upon me yet, but I knew not how passionately I loved you, until you became the wife of another. Isabel, I love you passionately still.

Isabel: How dare you presume to address me so?

Levison: What I have said can do no harm now; the time has gone by. We have each chosen our parts in life and must abide by them. The gulf between us is impassable, but the fault was mine. I ought to have avowed my affection for you, and not have suffered you to throw yourself away on Mr Carlyle.

Isabel: Do I hear aright? Throw myself away on Mr Carlyle, my husband — beloved, honoured and esteemed by all who know him! I married him of my own free choice and have never since regretted it. Look at his manly bearing, his noble mind, his generous nature. What are you in comparison? You forget yourself, Francis Levison!

"*Mr. Carlyle married Lady Isabel Vane*"

BARBARA *and* ISABEL   *Act III Scene II*

"She is dead, Miss Carlyle"

CORNELIA *and* LORD MOUNTSEV
Act III Scene II

"*I am ɪ
on the
threshol.
of the
next wo*

ISABEL
and
ARCHIE

*Act II
Scene II*

Levison: No, I do not. My intentions are strictly honourable. Am I not a man of my word?

Isabel: You are talking to me as you have no right to talk. Who but you would so insult me?

Levison: I have a right — that of my deep, my undying love.

Isabel: Must I remind you that you are here as the guest of him whose wife you insult by such behaviour. The roof which shelters you should be my protection.

Levison: I ask your pardon, Lady Isabel. I have acknowledged my fault. I can do no more. I shall not offend you again. But there are moments when our heart's dearest feelings break through the rules of life and betray themselves in spite of our sober judgement. But I see I must leave you now; so adieu. (*To french window before turning*) No, Lady Isabel, not adieu — but au revoir. (*Exit*).

Isabel: Oh, how can I ever tell my husband that this man, whom he has befriended and sheltered from the law, has thus dared to speak to me of love! Heaven only knows what the consequences would be. (*To down centre*) No! No! I cannot tell him; yet I feel I ought to tell him all. Yes — yes — I will seek him instantly, my good, my kind, my noble husband. (*Exit up right*).

Enter WILSON *and* JOYCE *from right.* WILSON *is carrying a small brush and pan for cleaning the hearth. She goes to the fireplace,* JOYCE *has flowers which she arranges in vases on the piano and down left table during the following scene.*

Wilson: So, that Francis Levison is to stay at East Lynne and I am to prepare his rooms for him.

Joyce: Then you'd better start as soon as you have cleaned up that hearth. You would not want to offend the mistress. (*Moves to piano*).

Wilson: How ill she looks — her ladyship. She looks to me as though she has not long for this world.

Joyce: Nonsense, Wilson! She was very ill when the last child was born but she is getting over it quickly now.

Wilson: My goodness wouldn't somebody's hopes be up again if anything should happen?

Joyce: Nonsense!

Wilson (*rising with the brush in her hand and turning to face* JOYCE): You may cry out 'nonsense' for ever, Joyce, but they would. And she would snap him up to a dead certainty. She'd never let him escape her a second time. She is as much in love with him as ever she was.

Joyce: It was all talk and fancy. Mr Carlyle never cared for her.

Wilson: If you'd lived in the Hare family, as I did for seven years before I came here, you'd have seen and heard things enough, I can tell you. I've seen him kiss her. Why, he gave her that locket and chain she wears, with a lock of his hair in it too. She has hardly had it off her neck since. My belief is that she wears it in her sleep.

Joyce (*moving down to table left*): More simpleton she! How thoroughly stupid she must have been to go on loving a man who didn't care for her.

Wilson (*resuming her brushing of hearth*): I tell you, Joyce, you don't know that he didn't care. You remember that day, just after the wedding, when Miss Barbara came to pay a visit?

Joyce: I remember it.

Wilson: Well, I was just on the point of coming in to this very room when I heard Mr Carlyle talking to Miss Hare. They were alone in here together.

Joyce: And, I suppose, you listened?

Wilson (*standing up and moving towards* JOYCE): I did that. (*in a stage whisper*) Miss Barbara was crying, sobs breaking from her like one might expect to hear from a breaking heart. It seemed as if she had been reproaching him, as if some explanation had passed and I heard him say that from henceforth they could only be brother and sister.

Joyce: She is a downright fool to suffer herself to love him still!

Wilson: But if Mr Carlyle should ever get tired of my lady and —

Joyce: Wilson! Have the goodness to recollect yourself!

Wilson: What have I said now? All I say is that if anything should happen to my lady, Miss Barbara, as sure as fate, would step into her shoes.

Joyce (*finishing the flowers*): Nothing is going to happen to her.

Wilson: I hope it is not — now or later for the sake of the dear children. Barbara Hare wouldn't make a very kind stepmother. Hating the mother as she does, the children would receive no love and —

Joyce (*firmly*): I tell you, Wilson, if you think to pursue these sort of topics at East Lynne, I shall inform my lady that you are no longer suited to the situation here. And now, if you've finished that hearth, you can get about your business and prepare those rooms for Captain Levison.

> WILSON *and* JOYCE *exit right. After they have gone the double doors, which were left slightly ajar, open slowly and* ISABEL *enters. She moves slowly down left.*

Isabel: Oh, misery, misery! Oh, how palpable to all eyes must be that woman's love for my husband! Palpable indeed when all East and West Lynne are talking of it and even my servants daily gossip over it and extend their pity to me. Oh, I cannot bear it — I cannot bear it! The thought will drive me frantic.

> ARCHIBALD *enters right.* ISABEL *sees him at once and runs across to meet him upstage of the sofa.*

Isabel: Oh, Archibald, promise me that you will not marry her! Archibald, promise it!

Archibald: I will promise you anything within reason, but I do not know what you mean. There is no possibility of my marrying anyone, Isabel, — you are my wife.

Isabel: But if I die? I may, you know I may, and many think I shall — do not let her usurp my place.

Archibald: Indeed she shall not — whoever you may be talking of. What have you been dreaming? Who it is that is troubling your mind? Come, sit down on the sofa by my side and you shall tell me. (*They sit —* ARCHIBALD *on the right*).

Isabel: Do I need to tell you? Do you need to ask? Did you love no one before you married me? Perhaps you have loved her since — perhaps you love her still?

Archibald (*earnestly*): Of whom do you speak, Isabel?

Isabel: Of Barbara Hare.

Archibald: Isabel, what notion you can have picked up about myself and Barbara Hare I am unable to conceive. I never entertained the faintest shadow of love for her, either before my marriage or since.

Isabel: But she loved you.

Archibald (*after a slight hesitation*): If it was so, Isabel, she was more reprehensibly foolish than I should have given her good sense credit for. A woman may almost as well lose herself as suffer herself to love unsought. If she did give her love to me, I can only say I was utterly unconscious of it. Believe me, you have as much cause to be jealous of Cornelia as you have of Barbara Hare.

Isabel: Oh, I will believe you, Archibald. It is but a foolish thought. I will banish it for ever from my mind.

Archibald: And now tell me what put this into your brain?

Isabel (*aside*): I cannot tell him I was foolish enough to listen to the gossip of the servants. He would despise me for it. (*Aloud*) I cannot tell you, Archibald.

Archibald: Has anyone been striving to bias your mind against me?

Isabel: Archibald, no! Would anyone dare to do it?

Archibald: Then did you dream — and could not forget it on awaking?

Isabel: I do sometimes dream strange things, especially in my feverish afternoon sleeps. I think I am a little delirious at times, Archibald, and do not know what is real and what is fancy.

Archibald: Do not heed any more of these dreams if you can help it. Regard them for what they are — illusions, neither pleasant for you nor fair to me. I am bound to you by fond ties as well as by legal ones, remember, Isabel, and it is out of Barbara Hare's power to step in between us.

Isabel: I will try, dear Archibald. I will trust you. (*Aside*) Yes, I will trust him. If not in whom can I trust? (*Aloud*) I will leave you now — I am fatigued and would retire to my own room. (*Rises and exits up right*).

Archibald (*centre stage*): What can have put this by-gone nonsense into my wife's head?

CORNELIA *enters right and crosses to* ARCHIBALD *centre stage*.

Cornelia: Archibald, I wish to speak to you in regard to that Francis Levison. I do not like either his appearance or his manners.

Archibald: Cornelia, he is my guest, and as such must be treated with respect.

Cornelia: With respect indeed! He is a good-for-nothing villain if I'm any judge of character and I don't care how soon you tell him to go.

Archibald: He will only be here for a few days. If Sir Peter is in the humour to discharge his claims, and the moment his resolve is known the ex-captain may walk Her Majesty's dominions an unmolested man, free to go where he will.

Cornelia: That may be, but why should he come to our house?

Archibald: My house, Cornelia — do not forget that. I proposed it myself. I had no idea you would dislike his coming. Why should you?

Cornelia: I do not like Francis Levison and no good will come of his visit here — mark my words. (*Exit right*).

After she has gone BARBARA *appears at the window*.

Barbara (*calling softly*): Archibald!

Archibald (*turning and seeing her*) (*Aside*): Barbara! How inopportune a moment for a visit! (*Aloud*) Barbara, how nice of you to pay us a social visit. Come in, do.

Barbara (*coming to centre stage*): I must, in all honesty, confess that the nature of my visit is not for social reasons.

Archibald: Really? What then?

Barbara: I have a matter of great importance to discuss with you. Is there anywhere we can talk without fear of being overheard?

Archibald: Come, sit on the sofa. You shall tell me here.

BARBARA *sits on the sofa and* ARCHIBALD *in the chair down right*.

Barbara (*after she is seated*): I hardly know how to begin. It concerns my brother.

Archibald: Richard!

Barbara: Alas, yes! As you know it is many years since I saw him last.

Archibald: I know that only too well.

Barbara: But I have seen him again — last night.

Archibald: How? Where?

Barbara: The clock had just struck ten. I was seated by the window looking across the lawn admiring the view by moonlight when I thought I saw someone at the far end of the lawn, just in advance of the shade of the trees. It was not their leaves that was causing the movement for it was a still night. I waited for several minutes and then I could faintly discern the outline of a human figure signalling me. My first thought was to alarm the servants, my second to be still for I remembered the fear and mystery that attached to the house.

Archibald: And then?

Barbara: I went into the hall, shut my mother in the parlour, and stood in the shade of the portico, gazing still. The figure had evidently followed my movements for he removed his hat and waved it violently. I returned to the parlour and collected my shawl and told my mother I would walk down the path. The beckoning figure retreated within the dark trees as I neared it. I halted and called out "Who and what are you? What do you want?"

Archibald: And it was Richard?

Barbara: Yes. He was dressed as a farm labourer. But in spite of his smock, his straw-wisped hat and his false whiskers, I knew him for my brother. I told him of the risk he was running in coming there, but he said he must run the risk for he could not go on living as he was then.

Archibald: Did he tell you where he was living?

Barbara: Yes, he was working in London in a stable yard. He was earning twelve shillings a week. He said he felt safer there in such obscurity — safer from the police runners.

Archibald: He must have committed the deed in madness.

Barbara: He swears he did not commit the deed at all. He swore to me that he was innocent of the crime.

Archibald: Then who could it have been that was responsible for the murder?

Barbara: He says it was a man named Thorn.

Archibald: Thorn? Who is Thorn?

Barbara: Richard says he was a friend of Afy's — though how he could come to mention that girl's name in my presence I do not know.

Archibald: And then?

Barbara: Then he begged me to be allowed an interview with Mama. He wanted a hundred pounds. He said he has the opportunity of doing better for himself and needs the money. I told him to come back tonight at eleven and that, in the meantime, I would speak to Mama and that the money would, no doubt, be his.

Archibald: And he agreed?

Barbara: He agreed. Then I implored him to try to prove his innocence. He said the evidence was too strong against him. Besides, no one at West Lynne knew anything about Thorn but Richard. It seems that Thorn only came over on certain nights to see — that girl, and took precious good care to keep out of the way in the daytime. Now, Archibald, we come to that part of the story which affects you.

Archibald: Affects me? In what way?

Barbara: I suggested to Richard that he told the whole truth to you. If anyone can help him, or take measures to establish his innocence — you can.

Archibald: I see. (*Rises*).

Barbara: Will you help him — please?

Archibald: When did you promise to give him my answer?

Barbara: Tonight, when he returns at eleven for the hundred pounds.

Archibald: Then you may also give him my solemn promise that I will do everything within my power to aid him.

Barbara (*rising and moving to* ARCHIBALD): Oh, Archibald you are very kind to us. You have ever treated me like a dear sister, and Mama is grateful to you for all your attentions to her. I fear we can never repay you sufficiently.

Archibald: I have only done what I felt to be my duty in the matter. Come, now, you are not to worry. I will escort you to the gate.

BARBARA *takes his arm and they go out through the french window. At the same time* ISABEL *and* LEVISON *enter up stage right.* ISABEL *crosses to the the window and looks out.*

Isabel (*aside*): That woman here — in privacy with my husband — under my very roof too. Ah then, 'tis true! My husband no longer loves me.

Levison (*crossing to right of* ISABEL): Who the deuce is that Barbara Hare? She is a devilish pretty girl. She seems to have a good understanding with your husband.

Isabel (*turning to face* LEVISON): What did you say, sir?

Levison: Nothing. I only spoke of monsieur, your husband. I meant not to offend.

Enter JOYCE *right. She comes centre.*

Joyce: If you please, my lady, little Isabel wishes to retire for the night and she wants you to kiss her before going to sleep.

Isabel (*crossly*): Tell the nurse to put the child to bed, and leave me.

Joyce: Yes, my lady. I'm sorry, my lady. (*Returns to door right — aside*) What! Put the child to bed without even saying goodnight! There's something strange going on here. (*Exit*).

Levison: By the bye, Lady Isabel, don't *you* think that Barbara Hare a devilish pretty girl?

Enter CORNELIA *right.*

Cornelia: Lady Isabel might I have the pleasure of a few words with you — alone.

Levison: I was just going. (*Bows*) Ladies — your servant. (*Exit window*).

Cornelia: How I dislike that man. (*Moving centre*).

Isabel (*coldly*): Is that what you came in here to say?

Cornelia: No. I came to tell you that I have taken the liberty of countermanding the order for little Isabel's new frock. I think she has enough already and does not require this one.

Isabel: She does require it. I am a competent judge of what is necessary for my own children.

Cornelia: She no more requires a new frock than that table requires one or than you require the one you are looking for. She has ever so many lying by, and her striped silk, turned, will make up as handsome as ever.

Isabel (*moving to* CORNELIA): Countermanding my orders, Miss Carlyle, is a liberty you have taken a great deal too often. Allow me to tell you that for the future I will be mistress in my own house.

Enter ARCHIBALD *through the french window.*

Cornelia: Archibald, what did Barbara Hare want?

Archibald: She wanted to see me on some business, that is all.

Cornelia: What rubbish, Archibald. As if you could not say outright what Barbara wants, without making a mystery of it. She seems to be always wanting you now. It is — it is never that old affair is being reaped up again?

Archibald: Cornelia, you will oblige me by not referring to that again.

Cornelia: Oh, indeed! Very well, very well. (*At door right — aside*) I trust they will listen to me when they are brought to ruin through Lady Isabel's extravagance. Poor Archibald, he works like a horse, and with all his slaving, can scarcely keep expenses down. (*Exit right*).

Isabel: Archibald, what *did* that woman — that Barbara Hare want here?

Archibald: It is private business, Isabel. She brought me a message from her mother.

Isabel: Must the secret be kept from me?

Archibald: It would not make you happier to know it, Isabel. There is a dark secret, you are aware, touching the Hare family. It is connected with that. Further I cannot tell you. I have taken a solemn vow to disclose to no one the nature of the business.

Isabel: I see. (*Moves away to below left end of sofa*).

Archibald: By the way, Isabel, I very much regret that I shall be unable to accompany you to the dinner party this evening. You must make my excuses to Mrs Jeafferson.

Isabel (*after a pause*): Why so?

Archibald (*coming down to her left*): Some business has arisen which I am compelled to attend to this evening. As soon as I have snatched my dinner at home, I must hasten back to the office. You must not be vexed, Isabel. I assure you it is no fault of mine. It is important private business which cannot be put off.

Isabel: You never return to the office in the evening.

Archibald: No, because if anything occurs to take us there after hours, my clerk officiates. But the business tonight must be done by myself.

Isabel: Shall you join us later in the evening?

Archibald: I believe I shall not be able to. I trust you will enjoy the party. I will see you when you return. Farewell. (*Exit up right*).

Isabel (*running up to double doors and calling after him*): Archibald! Archibald! (*Coming back into the room and closing the doors and leaning against the frame*) What mystery can they have between them that he dares not reveal to me, his wife? He is deceiving me — I am certain of that. Oh, I am wretched, jealous, mad.

LEVISON *enters at the french window.*

Levison (*aside*): I wonder what the duece that Hare girl can want with Carlyle. I followed them down to the gate and overheard them planning a meeting here this evening whilst Lady Isabel is at the party. Perhaps Lady Isabel would like to be present at that meeting also. (*Aloud*) Ah, still alone I see, Lady Isabel. I expected to find you so. I suspect that Mr Carlyle is more agreeably engaged.

Isabel: Engaged — in what manner, sir?

Levison (*moving to* ISABEL): As I came up the lawn, a few minutes since, I saw a lady and gentleman enjoying a tête-à-tête. I followed them to the gate, and overstepped the bounds of good manners so far as to listen to part of their conversation. I heard them arrange a meeting in this very room for this evening and, unless I am very much mistaken, the favoured individual was Mr Carlyle.

Isabel: My husband? Oh, sir, you cannot mean that! Oh, if I thought him capable of such a falsehood to me, I would leave his roof at once.

Levison: That's right; be avenged on the false hound. He never was worthy of your love. Leave your home of misery and come to one of happiness. Come, let me prove his perfidy to you.

Isabel: Only prove this and I will quit this house for ever!

Levison: With me, Isabel?

Isabel: Yes — with you. (*Aside*) If this be true then I care not who shall be the instrument of my vengeance.

CURTAIN

ACT TWO

SCENE TWO

LATER THE SAME EVENING. ARCHIBALD *is seated in the armchair down right looking at some papers. There is a knocking at the french window. He goes and opens it carrying the papers.*

Archibald: Who is there?
Richard (*off*): 'Tis I — Richard Hare — are you alone?
Archibald: Come in. We will not be disturbed. Lady Isabel is at a party and my sister has retired for the night.

RICHARD HARE *enters. He is a young man in his late twenties. He is rather thin. He is dressed as a farm labourer.* ARCHIBALD *closes the curtains and moves down to the table left. He pulls out the upstage chair.*

Archibald: Sit here, Richard, and you can tell me all that happened on that lamentable night.

RICHARD *sits in the upstage chair and* ARCHIBALD *in the chair left of the table.*

Richard: Thank you, you are very kind.
Archibald: Now tell me everything — in as few words as possible.
Richard: Well — there was a row at home about my going so much to Hallijohn's. The governor and my mother thought I went after Afy. Perhaps I did, perhaps I didn't. Hallijohn had asked me to lend him my gun, and that evening, when I went to see Af — when I went to see someone — never mind —
Archibald: Richard, there's an old saying and it's sound advice 'Tell the whole truth to your lawyer and your doctor.' If I am to judge whether anything can be attempted for you, you must tell me the whole truth without reserve. It shall be a sacred trust.
Richard: Then if I must, I must. I did love the girl. I would have waited till I was my own master to make her my

44

wife, though it had been for years and years. I could not do so then, you understand, in the face of my father's opposition.

Archibald: Your wife?

Richard: Why, you don't suppose I meant anything else! I would not have been such a blackguard.

Archibald: Well, go on, Richard. Did she return your love?

Richard: I can't be certain. Sometimes I thought she did, sometimes not. Anyway, on the night in question I went to the house to take my gun. Hallijohn was out so I gave it to Afy who opened the door. She would not let me go inside the house as usual. This made me mad with jealousy for I was sure that Thorn was in the cottage with her although she strongly denied it.

Archibald: Who was Thorn? I never heard of him.

Richard: Neither did anyone else, in West Lynne. He took care that it remained that way. He lived some miles away and used to come over in secret.

Archibald: Courting Afy?

Richard: Yes — courting her.

Archibald: Well, go on with your story of what happened that night.

Richard: When she refused me admittance, I determined to wait and find out for myself who was in the cottage with her. I hid myself in some trees near the house where I could see all that went on. After a while I saw Hallijohn come up the path near to where I was hiding, and go into the house. Not long afterwards, twenty minutes perhaps, I heard a shot and very soon, almost in the same minute, as it seemed, Thorn came panting and tearing along the path leading from the cottage. His appearance startled me. I had never seen a man show more utter terror. His face was livid, his eyes seemed staring, and his lips were drawn back from his teeth. Had I been a strong man, I should surely have attacked him. I was mad with jealousy for then I saw that Afy had sent me away that she might entertain him. He flew along swiftly, and I, afterwards heard the sound of his horse's hooves galloping away.

Archibald: Did you know where this Thorn lived?

Richard: I could never ascertain. Afy said he lived ten miles distant. He used to ride over once or twice a week to see her. I always thought he came under a false name. He appeared to be an aristocrat though of very bad taste. He made a great display of jewellery, expensive too — such as diamonds.

Archibald: What happened after Thorn had ridden away?

Richard: I ran to the house, leaped up the steps and — and — I fell over the prostrate body of Hallijohn. He was lying just within, on the kitchen floor — dead. Blood was around him, and my gun, discharged was thrown near him. I called Afy. No one answered. A sort of panic come over me — a fear. I could not have remained another minute with that dead man had it been to save my own life. I caught up the gun, and was making off when —

Archibald: Why did you catch up the gun?

Richard: Some sort of vague notion flashed on my brain that my gun ought not to be found near the murdered body of Hallijohn and so I seized it and rushed out just as people began to gather and, to my horror, I was taken for the murderer. I threw down the gun and fled.

Archibald: And that act alone condemned you. You acted like a guilty man, and that line of action often entails as much trouble as real guilt.

Richard: Alas — only too true but who would believe my story now?

Archibald: Richard, where is Afy now?

Richard: How should I know? I was going to ask you.

Archibald: She disappeared immediately after the funeral and it was thought — in short, Richard, the neighbourhood gave her credit for having gone after and joined you.

Richard: What a pack of idiots! I have neither seen nor heard of her since that unfortunate night. If she went after anyone, it was after Thorn.

Archibald: Can you describe this man Thorn — was he good looking?

Richard: I suppose the world would call him so. He had shining black hair and whiskers, dark eyes and handsome features. But his vain dandyism spoilt him.

Archibald: I see. (*Rising*) And now you had better go. I will send a message to Barbara advising her when and where we can meet again. In the meantime I'll decide what course you are to adopt and how I can best serve you.

Richard (*rising*) Thank you again.

ARCHIBALD goes to the door up centre, goes into the hall, and returns.

Archibald: All is clear — you can go from here in safety.

Richard (*at the door*): Goodbye, good, kind friend.

They shake hands and RICHARD exits up left. ARCHIBALD returns into the room and closes the doors. He goes to the table and begins to collect up his papers.

Archibald: Now I must hasten to the Jeaffersons to fetch my dear Isabel. How I dislike not being able to take her into my confidence in this matter of Richard Hare but I have given my solemn promise and no power on earth or in Heaven would make me betray my trust.

There is a rapping at the window.

Archibald (*going to window*): Who can that be? (*Opens the window and BARBARA comes in*) Barbara, what brings you here?

Barbara: I was afraid that Richard might be discovered. I came to see him safely away from here. Where is he?

Archibald: He departed but a minute since. He will be safe in the darkness, never fear.

Barbara: Did he confide in you?

Archibald: He told me everything. I will do all in my power to assist him.

Barbara: Archibald, you are the kindest man in the whole world. How can I show to you the gratitude I feel within my heart?

Archibald (*taking her hand*): Dear Barbara, you have no need. And now — it is not politic that you should remain here. I will see you safely to your gate.

Barbara: That is not necessary, Archibald. It is but a few steps. I can go alone.

Archibald: Nonsense Barbara! I would not allow you to venture along the high road again at this hour.

Barbara: Very well.

Archibald: And on the way I can arrange with you the time and place when I can see Richard again. Come, take my arm. (*They go out through the french window*).

As they go out, the door upstage opens and ISABEL *and* LEVISON *enter. They come to below the sofa.*

Levison: There, Lady Isabel, I told you what you might see. This is the second time today we have come through that door and seen them together. Do you require further proof?

Isabel: With her! Then my fears were not unfounded.

Levison: You see now why he could not accompany you.

Isabel (*sinking on to the sofa*): Oh, you torture me!

Levison: You whom I have loved so constantly through all, through coldness and disdain on your part, through the helpless, hopeless misery I have endured in seeing you the wife of one who loves you as you see.

Isabel: (*turning to him fiercely*): Oh, why have you shown me this?

Levison: To prove how grossly you are deceived. Be avenged on him. Leave this life of doubts and fears; come to happiness with one whose love for you will never change.

Isabel: Tempt me not, leave me, I am almost mad!

Levison (*moving to window*): Look there again. Even from here I can see how he whispers in her ear, how close his lips are to hers. Come. (*Crosses to* ISABEL *and takes her to the window and forces her to look out*): Can you not, in imagination, hear the loving words that he should speak to none but you?

Isabel (*turning from the window*): It is too plain. He loves her and I — I —

Levison: Am deceived. Can you endure the sight of that and yet seek no revenge? Will you spurn my true love? Will you — oh say, dear Isabel — will you fly with me — fly from him who insults you thus?

Isabel: Yes — come weal, come woe, I will — — I will be avenged on him for so cruelly wronging me.

Levison: Come then, swift hands shall be in readiness and we —

Isabel: Go — I will rejoin you in a few minutes.

LEVISON exits up centre. ISABEL goes to the long table, takes pen, ink and paper and brings it to the table left. She sits in upstage chair and writes a letter.

Isabel (*when she has finished — rising*): Now, Francis Levison, I trust my future in your hands, and may Heaven forgive me.

JOYCE enters from right. She comes to ISABEL.

Joyce: Oh, my lady, are you ill?

Isabel: Aye — ill and wretched! Joyce, I want a promise from you. If anything should happen to me, remain at East Lynne with my children.

Joyce: I will stay with them. But oh, my lady, what can be the matter with you? Are you taken suddenly ill?

Isabel: Nothing can avail me now. I am beyond mortal aid. Goodbye, Joyce — remember your promise as you hope for mercy. (*Moves up to double doors and turns to JOYCE*) Goodbye. (*Exit*).

Joyce (*running up to door and calling*): My lady! My lady! My lady! (*Turning downstage*) What can she mean — when I am gone? Ah, I think I know what her wild looks, her sad, pale face and broken-acted tones meant. Merciful Heaven, where is Mr Carlyle? (*To centre stage*) Mr Carlyle! Mr Carlyle!

Enter ARCHIBALD at window.

Joyce (*running to him*): Oh, sir, sir, have you seen my lady?

Archibald: She has gone to Mrs Jeafferson. I am about to take the carriage to fetch her home.

Joyce (*turning away her head*): She has returned already.

Archibald: Returned?

Joyce: Yes — and gone — gone — to take the life that is not hers to take.

Archibald: Joyce, what do you mean?

Joyce (*turning to ARCHIBALD*): She has destroyed herself, sir, as true as we are living here. I can understand her words now. I could not before. Oh, sir, my lady has been miserably unhappy, and that has driven her to it. May Heaven support you under this dreadful trial.

Archibald: Joyce, are you in your senses or out of them? Your lady miserably unhappy! What do you mean by such an assertion?

Enter CORNELIA *up right. She is wearing a dressing gown. She comes to centre stage.*

Cornelia: Whatever's the matter?

Joyce: I am glad that you have come, ma'am, for what I was about to say to my master I would prefer to say in your presence. When my lady is brought into this house, and laid down before us, dead, what will your feelings be? My master has done his duty by her love, but you — (*moves to* CORNELIA) — you have made her life a misery. Yes, ma'am, you have!

Cornelia: Highty tighty! What is all this? Where's my lady?

Joyce: She has gone to destroy herself and I say she has been driven to it. She has not been allowed to indulge a will of her own, poor thing, since she came to East Lynne. In her own house she has been less free than one of her own servants. All these years she has been crossed and put upon — everything, in short, but beaten — ma'am, you know she has!

Archibald (*moving to* JOYCE): What is that you are saying, Joyce? I do not understand.

Joyce: I have longed to say it to you many a hundred times, sir, but it is right that you should hear it, now things have come to this dreadful ending. Since the very night Lady Isabel came home here, your wife, she has been taunted with the cost she has brought to East Lynne and you. If she wanted the simplest thing, she was forbidden to have it, and told she was bringing her husband to poverty. (*To* CORNELIA) I have seen her, ma'am, come away from your reproaches with tears in her eyes. A gentle-spirited, high-born lady, as she was, could not fail to be driven to desperation and I know that she has been.

Archibald (*moving down left*): May God forgive you, Cornelia! (*Sees letter on table left*) Ah, writing in her hand! Why do I fear to read? (*Opens the letter and reads*).

Voice of Isabel: When years go by and my children ask where their mother is, and why she left them, tell them that you, their father, goaded her to it. If they enquire what she is, tell them also, if you will, but tell them at the same time that you outraged and betrayed her, driving her to the depth of desperation ere she quitted them in her despair.

ARCHIBALD *slowly but deliberatly crumples up the letter in his hand. He stands staring into space.*

Joyce: Sir, does it say she is dead?
Archibald: She is not dead — worse than that. Had she died, I could still have worshipped, honoured her memory while I mourned her loss, but not now. My poor children, never, never will they see their mother more — never! Oh, God give me strength to bear this blow.
Joyce: Poor little William — poor little Isabel!
Archibald (*turning up to* JOYCE): Never let me hear you speak that name in this house again. Henceforth the child shall be called Lucy. Remember that and remember it well.
Cornelia: May God be merciful to this dishonoured house!

CURTAIN

ACT THREE

SCENE ONE

A WINTER'S EVENING SEVERAL YEARS LATER. *When the curtain rises* ARCHIBALD *is seated upstage of the table left writing.* CORNELIA *is seated on the right end of the sofa. She is suffering from a head cold. She sneezes.*

Archibald (*automatically*): God, bless you.

Cornelia: Archibald, what's the time I wonder?

Archibald (*looking at his watch*): Just nine, Cornelia.

Cornelia: Well then I think I'll go to bed and after I'm in it, I'll have a basin of arrowroot of gruel, or some slop of that sort. I'm sure I've been free enough all my life of wanting any such sick stuff.

Archibald: Well, do so, if you think it will do you any good.

Cornelia: Well there's one thing I know of that's excellent for a cold in the head and that is to take your red flannel petticoat and tie it on crosswise over your night-cap. I think I'll try it too. (*Rises*).

Archibald (*rising*): One minute, Cornelia, before you retire there is a matter of considerable importance with which I wish to aquaint you.

Cornelia: Importance? What can it be that is more important than my cold in the head. (*Sneezes*).

Archibald: Cornelia, please sit down again — this may take a little time.

Cornelia (*sitting*): Oh, very well, but please make it as brief as possible.

Archibald (*crossing and sitting beside her on her left*): I will try. Cornelia, when I married Lady Isabel Vane you reproached me severely with having kept you in the dark —

Cornelia (*fiercely*): If you had not kept me in the dark but consulted me, as any other Christian would, the course of events might have been wholly changed, and the wretchedness and disgrace that fell on this house would have been spared to it.

Archibald: Cornelia, do I have to remind you that Lady Isabel is no more?

Cornelia: Oh, I know that well enough. They do say that one should speak no evil of the dead, but what I say is that if she had not run away with that scoundrel Levison and if he had not deserted her, as I knew he would, then she would not have been alone in France and would not have been in that railway train when it crashed.

Archibald: We will leave the past and consider the future. I was about to remark that I do not intend to fall under your displeasure again for a similar offence. I believe you have never wholly forgiven it.

Cornelia: And never shall. I did not deserve the slight.

Archibald: Therefore, almost as soon as I know it myself, I aquaint you with the fact. Cornelia, I am about to marry for a second time.

Cornelia (*sneezing violently so that her spectacles drop off her nose and her knitting box clatters to the floor*): What did you say?

Archibald: I am about to marry.

Cornelia: You!

Archibald: I. Is there anything so very astonishing in it?

Cornelia: For the love of common sense don't go making such a fool of yourself! You have done it once; was that not enough for you, but you must run your head into the noose again?

Archibald: Now, Cornelia, can you wonder that I do not speak to you of such things, when you meet them in this way? You treat me just as you did when I was a child. (*Rising and moving left centre*) It is very foolish.

Cornelia: When folks act childishly they must be treated as children. I always thought you were mad when you married before, but I shall think you doubly mad now.

Archibald: Because you have preferred to remain single and solitary yourself, is it any reason why you should condemn me to do the same?

Cornelia (*angrily*): That she may go and disgrace you, as the last one did?

Archibald: No, I am not afraid of that, in the one I have chosen.

Cornelia: Pray — who is it that you have chosen? The whole neighbourhood has been after you.

Archibald: It is Barbara Hare.

Cornelia (*rising and shrieking*): Who?

Archibald: You are not deaf, Cornelia!

Cornelia: Well you *are* an idiot!

Archibald (*without irritation*): Thank you.

Cornelia (*going to him*): And so you are — *you are*, Archibald. To suffer that girl, who has been angling after you so long, to catch you at last.

Archibald: She has not angled after me. Whatever passing fancy she may have entertained for me in earlier days, she has shown no symptoms of it of late years.

Cornelia: She is a little conceited minx.

Archibald: What else have you to urge against her?

Cornelia: I would have married a girl without a slur upon her — if I must have married.

Archibald: Slur?

Cornelia: Yes. Is it an honour to possess a brother such as Richard?

Archibald: There is no slur upon Barbara. And the time may come when it will be taken from Richard.

Cornelia (*moving away right — sniffing*): Pigs may fly, but I never saw them do so.

Archibald: The next consideration, Cornelia, is about your residence. You will go back, I presume, to your own home.

Cornelia (*turning to him*): Go back to my own home! I shall do nothing of the sort. I shall stop at East Lynne. What's to hinder me?

Archibald (*decisively*): It cannot be.

Cornelia (*sharply*): Who says so?

Archibald: I do. Have you forgotten that night — when *she* went away — the words spoken by Joyce? Cornelia, whether they were true or false, I will not subject another to a similar chance. I cast no reflection upon you. You have been mistress of a house for many years, and you naturally expect to be so still. It is right that you should be. But two mistresses in one house do not answer, Cornelia; they never did and they never will.

Cornelia (*resentfully*): You will not find a better mistress of a house than I have made you.

Archibald: I do not expect to do so. (*Moving to her*) The tenants leave your house in March, do they not?

Cornelia: Yes, they do. Are you aware that in leaving your house, I take my income with me, Mr Archibald?

Archibald: Most certainly. Your income is yours, and you will require it for your own purposes. I have neither right to it, nor wish for it.

Cornelia: The withdrawal will make a pretty hole in your income, I can tell you that. Take care that you and East Lynne don't go bankrupt together. Now I will go to bed — my cold is much worse suddenly. (*Sneezes*) Who knows but that I might die of it — then you would have no need to throw me out, would you Archibald? (*Goes to double doors*).

Archibald: Cornelia, I have no wish to —

Cornelia: Goodnight, Archibald. (*Sneezes*) Barbara Hare — that extravagant, vain upstart little reptile. (*Exit*).

After she has gone, ARCHIBALD *crosses to the window and looks out.*

Archibald: I wonder if it snows still. (*Opens window*).

Richard (*off*): Let me come in, Mr Carlyle, for the love of life. I see you are alone. I'm dead beat; and I do not know but that I'm dodged also. (*He comes in*) Lock the door, sir; 'tis I, Richard Hare.

ARCHIBALD *crosses to the door right and locks it and then moves up to the double doors and locks them.*

Archibald: Richard, I am thunderstruck. I fear you have done wrong to come here. (*Going to him*) Come, sit by the fire and I will get you a drink. (*Takes* RICHARD *to right end of sofa and then goes up to long table*).

Richard (*seated*): I cut off from London at a moment's notice. I'm dodged, Mr Carlyle, I am indeed. The police are after me, set on by that wretch Thorn.

Archibald (*coming to right of* RICHARD *and handing him a glass of brandy*)   Take it, Richard, it will warm you. (*Takes glass*) How you tremble!

Richard: A few hours outside in the cold snow is enough to make the strongest man tremble, sir. And it lies so deep in some places that you have to come along at a snail's pace.

Archibald (*sitting in chair down right*): And you have walked all the way from London?

Richard: All the way. Even now the officers may be in pursuit. I had no money to pay for a lodging or even buy food. I waited outside the window till I saw you were alone. I have come to ask your advice.

Archibald: Have you then discovered this man Thorn?

Richard: Yes, about a week ago, for the first time, I got a glimpse of him as he was passing by in a carriage. I tried to follow him then but they drove too fast for me. The other evening I saw him again, standing in front of a theatre. He saw me, and in a moment, recognised me, for he turned deadly pale. Then he flew into a fierce passion, and swore that if he ever caught me near him again he would hand me over to the nearest officer. Then, yesterday, I saw him again at the entrance to Tattersalls. His face turned savage and he beckoned a policeman, pointed me out, and said something to him in a quick tone. I managed to get among the crowd again and fled as fast as possible. After that I knew I was no longer safe in London. Mr Carlyle — is this sort of life to go on with me for ever?

Archibald: I am deeply sorry for you, Richard. I wish I could remedy it. (*The double doors rattle.* RICHARD *jumps up*) Be still, be at ease, Richard. No one shall come in. It is only one of the servants, I expect.

Joyce (*off*): Miss Carlyle has left her handkerchief downstairs, sir, and has sent me for it.

Archibald (*rising and going to doors*): You cannot come in, I am busy.

Joyce: Very good, sir.

Richard: Who was it?

Archibald: It was Joyce.

Richard: Is she still here? (*Moving down centre*) Has anything ever been heard of Afy?

Archibald (*moving to left of* RICHARD): Afy was here two or three months ago.

Richard: Was she? What is she doing?

Archibald: She is in service. I questioned her about Thorn. She protested solemnly to me that it was not Thorn who committed the deed.

Richard: It *was* Thorn.

Archibald: Richard, you cannot tell. You did not see it done.

Richard: I know that no man could have rushed out in that frantic manner, with those signs of guilt and fear about him, unless he had been engaged upon some dreadful deed.

Archibald: Afy declares he was with her.

Richard: But Afy swore at the inquest that she was *alone* when the deed was done; that she was alone in the wood at the back of the cottage. Now that I have —

There is a loud knocking at the double doors.

Cornelia (*off*): Archibald, who have you got in that room?

Archibald (*going up to door*): It is someone on business. You cannot come in now. (*To* RICHARD *in a stage whisper*) It is only my sister, Richard. Be a man and shake off this fear. No harm shall come to you in my house. (*Moves to door right and unlocks it*) You had better retire till I have spoken to my sister.

RICHARD *crosses to door and exits.*

Cornelia (*off*): Archibald, are you there? Open the door I say!

ARCHIBALD *crosses to the upstage door and unlocks it.* CORNELIA *enters in her dressing gown with a red flannel petticoat tied round her head. She comes to centre stage.*

Cornelia: Where is she, I say? (*Turning up to* ARCHIBALD) Oh, you ought to be ashamed of yourself. I'd rather believe anything wicked of myself than of you, Archibald.

Archibald (*coming down to her left*): Why, what do you mean? I think your cold must have affected your reason. There has been no woman here but a man who fears the police are on his track. You ought to be able to guess his name.

Cornelia: What! Not Richard Hare? Let me see him. Where is he?

RICHARD *enters right*. CORNELIA *goes to him*.

Cornelia: Richard, what on earth brought you here? It's nothing short of madness.

Richard: The Bow Street runners were after me and I had to get away from London at a moment's notice. I had no money to pay for a lodging or to buy food, so I came to Mr Carlyle to befriend me.

Cornelia: It just serves you right. You would go hunting after that brazen hussy, Afy Hallijohn.

Archibald: Cornelia, this is no time for upbraidings. Do go and prepare him some food, while I see after his lodgings.

Cornelia: It is impossible for him to sleep here without it being known to Joyce. And I suppose Richard and Joyce are upon the friendly terms of daggers drawn, for she believes him to be the murderer of her father.

Richard: Let me disabuse her. Allow me to see her and convince her.

Cornelia: Plenty of time for that. Now let me see; there's that small room at the back of mine. You can sleep there. But Joyce must be taken into our confidence. Come along, Richard. I'll see what can be done for you. (*Crosses to door right*) You know you always were the greatest natural born fool that ever was let loose out of leading-strings.

Richard (*turning to* ARCHIBALD): Once more, sir, I am in your debt. How can I ever repay you for all you have done for me?

Archibald: Do not even mention it, Richard. One day we shall see you a free man and that shall be my reward.

RICHARD *and* CORNELIA *go off right and* ARCHIBALD *is returning to gather up his papers as*

THE CURTAIN FALLS

ACT THREE
SCENE TWO

EIGHTEEN MONTHS LATER. *At curtain rise* JOYCE *and* WILSON *are standing centre stage —* JOYCE *on the left.*

Wilson: I trust that Miss Carlyle isn't to stay here for more than a few days.

Joyce: That is no business of yours, Wilson.

Wilson: I hoped I'd seen the back of her when she went to live at West Lynne when the master married again.

Joyce: Have you nothing better to do than to stand here gossiping? I can find you plenty to do, with Miss Carlyle and Lord Mountsevern here as guests and the new governess arriving today.

Wilson: Well it's to hoped she's not full of airs and graces like the last one.

Joyce: Mrs Carlyle's friend, Mrs Latimer met her in Germany and has given her the highest recommendations. Now perhaps you will go and see that her room is prepared.

Wilson: Oh, very well. We musn't neglect Madame Whatshername must we?

Joyce: The new governess is called Madame Vine, Wilson, and there is no occasion to be insolent.

Wilson (*moving to door right*): I'm going. You worry too much, Joyce — the room will be ready.

Joyce: Well, just see that it is.

> WILSON *exits right as* LORD MOUNTSEVERN *and* CORNELIA *enter upstage right.*

Joyce: Good morning, my lord. Good morning ma'am. (*Exit right*).

Lord M (*moving to window and looking out*): So, you no longer reside at East Lynne.

Cornelia (*to left end of sofa*): No! I am now at my house at West Lynne. Since my brother was so foolish as to marry again I have taken up my old residence. Why couldn't he remain single as I have done?

Lord M: Well, ma'am, why should he? Marriage is a happy state — happy, honourable, and —

Cornelia (*sitting*): Very happy, very honourable. His first marriage brought him all that — did it not? Oh, I beg your pardon, I forgot that you were a relative of — of —. Tell me, my lord, was it a positively ascertained fact that Lady Isabel died after that terrible railway accident in France?

Lord M (*moving to left of* CORNELIA): She certainly did die, poor child! Did Carlyle not tell you of the letter she wrote to me on her death bed?

Cornelia: No! I never heard of any letter. May I ask the nature of it?

Lord M: The letter was to the effect that she was dying from the injuries she had received. She said she was glad to, and so deliver all who had ever loved her from the shame she had brought on them. I cannot recollect the exact words now but I can recall the last few lines. They were 'Go to Mr Carlyle, say that I humbly beg him to forgive me; tell him that I repent the wrong I have done him'. The final words I can remember only too well 'I can write no more, my bodily pain is so great, but no greater than my mental agony and remorse — farewell, forgive me for my shame — Isabel'.

Cornelia: Poor, erring creature! Heaven be merciful to her.

Lord M: Alas, poor child, she has gone beyond all doubt. Why did you ask?

Cornelia: A thought came over me, today, to wonder whether she was really dead.

Lord M: She is dead, Miss Carlyle. And now I must seek out your brother. There is a matter I have to discuss with him in connection with his nomination.

Cornelia: Nomination?

Lord M: To parliament. Do not tell me he has not confided in you.

Cornelia (*rising*): Archibald Carlyle in parliament — what next? You had better to nominate him for the County Lunatic Asylum than that idle, do-nothing House of Commons. Have you thought of the cost, pray?

Lord M: Oh, that's a mere nothing. It's not worth naming.

Cornelia: Oh that ever I should live to hear money talked of as not worth naming.

Enter ARCHIBALD *and* BARBARA *up centre. They come to centre stage.*

Cornelia: Archibald, have you completely given leave to your senses? Parliament indeed!

Lord M: Carlyle, may I have a word with you?

Archibald: Certainly. Barbara dear, perhaps you would entertain my sister.

Cornelia: Psha!

LORD MOUNTSEVERN *and* ARCHIBALD *go over left to the table and* BARBARA *sits on the sofa with* CORNELIA. BARBARA *on the left.*

Lord M: Carlyle, who do you think has had the audacity to come to West Lynne, and set himself up as a candidate in opposition to you?

Archibald: A second man? Let him come on. We shall have the satisfaction of knowing who wins in the end. Well, who is this formidable apponent?

Lord M: Mr — or as he is now, Sir Francis Levison.

Barbara (*rising*): Archibald, you will not suffer this insolent man to deter you from your plans? You will not withdraw?

Archibald (*coming to centre stage*): Certainly not, Barbara. He has thrust himself offensively upon me in this measure and I think my better plan will be to take no more notice of him than if he were the dirt under my feet.

Barbara: Quite right, quite right, my husband.

Cornelia (*rising*): I should think so too. I was averse to it before but now I withdraw all my objections. In fact I'll give you a thousand pounds myself for ale for the electors.

Archibald: Keep your money, sister. It will not be needed.

Cornelia: Well, I've heard of a Lady Somebody who kissed a blacksmith to ensure her husband's election. Now I'm sure I'd kiss every man in East and West Lynne, blacksmiths included, to ensure your election. And now, I must return home. Remember, Archibald, take no more notice of that Levison than if he were a viper.

Archibald: Do not worry, Cornelia — farewell and thank you.

Barbara: I will see you to your carriage, Cornelia.

CORNELIA *and* BARBARA *exit up right centre.*

Lord M: I fear that I also must be going. Carlyle, you will not be driven from the field by — him. You'll face him and —

Archibald: Face him! Yes — yes —

Lord M: That's right. I'll bring my influence to bear. Ugh, the scoundrel, if duelling had been legal, I would have shot him like a dog. Don't bother to see me out, Carlyle. Goodbye.

They shake hands and LORD MOUNTSEVERN *goes out up left.* ARCHIBALD *moves down right.*

Archibald: Levison here! Oh, how the bitter memory of my irreparable wrong makes heart and brain burn with a mad, wicked desire for vengeance on the head of that man who brought shame and death on her whom I loved. Oh, Isabel, when I think of your untimely fate, I feel that this life would be a just sacrifice to your dear shade. But I dare not break a holier vow than any made by man. I dare not disobey the voice of the Omnipotent who hath said 'Vengeance is mine alone, I will repay'. To His eternal justice I leave the punishment of the wretched man who dishonoured my name and betrayed my poor, lost Isabel.

BARBARA *enters up right and crosses down to* ARCHIBALD'S *left.*

Barbara: Archibald, I fear I may have done a foolish thing.

Archibald: I fear we all do sometimes. Tell me, dearest.

Barbara: It is something I have had on my mind for months. You remember that night that Richard came here to see you? I mean the night that — that Lady Isabel quitted East Lynne.

Archibald: I remember.

Barbara: Richard came back to me again after he had left us. I was standing by the open window and he motioned me out to him. He told me that he had just met the real Thorn in the lane. He described a peculiar motion of the hand as he constantly threw back the hair from his brow, and he also spoke of the diamond ring — how it glittered in the moonlight. Archibald, I know not how to say this. Since that time — I have had a firm belief that Thorn is — is the same person as Levison.

Archibald: Levison! Why did you not mention this before?

Barbara: I did not like to remind you of that night before, but today, I saw Sir Francis Levison addressing a crowd of people in the street. I did not know why at the time — although the reason is now obvious. Whilst he was talking, there was the old action of the hand that Richard had described. I have written to Richard to steal down here, and try, if possible, to discover his identity. The letter is gone.

Archibald: Well, we must shelter him as best we can.

Barbara: Archibald, dear Archibald, what can be done to clear him?

Archibald: I cannot act against Levison.

Barbara: Not act — not act for Richard?

Archibald: My dearest, how can I? It would look like revenge.

Barbara: Forgive me — you are always right. But what steps can be taken?

Archibald: It is a case encompassed with difficulties. Let us wait until Richard arrives.

Barbara: As you wish, dearest Archibald.

Archibald: Spoken like my own wife. And now you must sing for me, Barbara.

Barbara (*crossing to the piano*): I have been learning another song. I had meant to practice it more before I sang it to you but I will wait no longer. (*Sits at piano*).

Archibald (*crossing to the right of the piano*): Sing it for me, dearest.

She sings 'The years that pass away' as ISABEL *did at the end of act one. While she is singing,* ISABEL *enters right, She is greatly changed. Her hair is white and she wears dark glasses. She walks with a limp. She remains at the door until the song has ended.*

Barbara (*rising and moving to down centre*): Ah, this is Madame Vine I believe, our new governess. Please to step this way, Madame Vine. I hope you are not tired after your journey. You are not ill are you?

ISABEL *comes across to* BARBARA *centre stage.*

63

Isabel: Not ill, madame, — only a little fatigued.

Archibald: I'll leave you to arrange matters between your-selves. (*Aside*) I've seen those features before, I'm certain of it — but where can it have been? (*Exit up right*).

Barbara: Do please be seated, Madame Vine. Or perhaps you would prefer to retire to bed at once and leave the interview until the morning.

Isabel: I would rather we talked now, madame.

Barbara: Very well. (*Takes the chair from upstage of the table and places it centre stage*). Please sit here, Madame Vine.

Isabel: Thank you.

Barbara (*sitting on left end of sofa*): Mrs Latimer wrote us word that you would be quite sure to suit us. I hope you will and that you will find your residence here agreeable. Have you lived much in England?

Isabel: In the early portion of my life.

Barbara: And you have lost your husband and children? Stay — I beg your pardon if I am making a mistake. I think Mrs Latimer did mention children.

Isabel (*faintly*): I have lost them.

Barbara: You are, no doubt, aware that these children you will have charge of are not mine. They are the children of Mr Carlyle's first wife.

Isabel: She is dead, I hear.

Barbara: Mr Carlyle married Lady Isabel Vane. She was attractive and beautiful but I do not fancy she cared very much for her husband. She ran away from him.

Isabel: It was very sad.

Barbara: Sad? It was wicked and infamous. She eloped with Francis Levison. They lived together in France until he deserted her when he had tired of her — villain that he is.

Isabel: Indeed so.

Barbara: Of course, the disgrace is reflected on the children.

Isabel: Do they ever allude to her?

Barbara: In conversation, from time to time, Wilson tells me; but I would recommend you, Madame Vine, not to encourage them in that. They had better forget her. I trust you will be able to instil principles into the little girl which will keep her from a like fate.

Isabel: I will try. Do the children enjoy good health, may I ask?

Barbara: Quite — except for the eldest boy, William. He has a bad cough and Mr Carlyle fears that he may not be long for this world.

Isabel (*aside*): William ill! Oh, no! (*Aloud*) How does Mr Carlyle bear the thought of parting with him?

Barbara: Bravely, Madame Vine. Mr Carlyle is not the man to betray emotions whatever his feelings may be. Even when Lady Isabel left him he made no outward sign of grief although it must have wrung his very heart strings.

Isabel: Ay, madame, because he did not love her truly; his best love was given to another.

Barbara: That is nonsense. Who told you that? She was his heart's idol. Mr Carlyle is a man who always speaks the truth, and he told me, in confidence, that he would never have married again during Lady Isabel's lifetime. It was a shocking affair all through. Poor Lady Isabel! Could she have forseen her fate, she would never have taken such a rash step, or had she known what a villain Levison was. Not only is he a bad man in principle but he is a murderer.

Isabel: Oh, no! (*Rising*) No, not a murderer. A bad man, a very bad man — but not a murderer!

Barbara: Oh, did you know him then?

Isabel: No, I did not know him, madame, but I have heard the story.

Barbara: His guilt has not been proved but I feel confident, in my own mind, that it soon will be.

Enter JOYCE *right with a letter. She comes down to right of* BARBARA.

Joyce: My lady, here's a letter which has been sent by a special messenger. (*Exit right*).

Barbara (*aside*): Ah, this is from my brother, Richard, to inform me of his coming. I must go and see my husband at once. (*Aloud*) (*Rising*) Madame Vine, I must beg you to excuse me for the present. I am called away by some important duties. Make yourself perfectly at home in my absence. East Lynne is small and I've no doubt you'll soon become familiar with it. (*Exit up right*).

Isabel (*moving about the room*): Familiar with East Lynne! Did she but know how familiar East Lynne is to me! What will be my trials now? To see him, my husband once, caress the woman I hate, to be compelled to witness the thousand little proofs of affection that were once bestowed upon me, to see his love for her child, whilst I must teach my own children to forget my memory. Oh, why did I come here? Why place myself in such daily torments? Oh, Isabel, Isabel — patience — patience! It is thus you bear your cross in life.

CURTAIN

ACT THREE

SCENE THREE

A MONTH LATER. CORNELIA *is seated on the sofa right*. JOYCE *is standing on her left*.

Cornelia: A fine row we had in the town, Joyce this afternoon. The villagers gave Francis Levison a ducking in the pond. Perhaps now he'll realise he's wasting his time opposing Mr Carlyle as candidate for West Lynne.

Joyce: Serve him right if they had let him drown! I have heard of it ma'am. Squire Pinner's ploughman called in here and told us the news. I never saw a man so excited. He said it was he who held one leg when they soused him in. Afy saw it — if you'll excuse me mentioning her name to you ma'am — and when she came in here she fell into hysterics.

Cornelia: Whatever for?

Joyce: It upset her so.

Cornelia: Upset her? Why should it upset her? It wouldn't have done any harm it they'd ducked her as well. What did she come here for, anyway?

Joyce: She came with a message from Mrs Latimer to Madame Vine.

Cornelia: Joyce, of whom does the new governess put you in mind?

Joyce (*quietly*): There are times when she puts me in mind of my late lady, both in face and manner.

Cornelia: Have you ever seen her without her glasses?

Joyce: No, never.

Cornelia: I did today, and I can tell you, Joyce, that I was confounded at the likeness. One would think it was the ghost of Lady Isabel Vane come into this world again.

Joyce: Oh, ma'am!

Cornelia: By the by, what is this I hear about William being worse? If I am to believe what I hear, he is in a very bad way indeed.

Joyce: Yes, ma'am, he is very ill. Madame Vine is with him now.

67

Cornelia: I shouldn't be surprised if he did drop off. He is his mother again all over, so far as constitution goes, and I'm sure she was never good for much.

Joyce: I wouldn't agree with that ma'am; but I do know that Madame Vine herself is far from well. She has been coughing badly these past few days. She scarcely had the strength to climb the stairs to Master William's bedroom this afternoon. I begged her to lie down and allow me to stay with Master William but she flatly refused and said her place was with him to the end.

Enter WILSON *right in great excitement. She runs across to* JOYCE *centre.*

Wilson: Joyce! Joyce! (*Seeing* CORNELIA) Begging your pardon, ma'am, but I'm that excited.

Cornelia: And what could possibly excite you, Wilson, sufficiently to enable you to forget your place?

Wilson: I'm sorry, ma'am, but it's Sir Francis Levison and Otway Bethel. They are arrested for the wilful murder of Hal — of your father, Joyce.

Joyce: What? What was that you said?

Wilson: Levison was the man who did it and young Richard Hare has been innocent all along. The officers have put handcuffs on Francis Levison and taken him off.

Cornelia: Then I trust he will have a pleasant journey to prison. Richard Hare innocent after all!

Enter ARCHIBALD, BARBARA *and* RICHARD *from the french window.*

Archibald (*as he comes into the room*): Yes, innocent. He can now walk abroad in the light of day, for the proofs of his innocence are so overwhelming that he can enter a court of justice without fear.

WILSON *and* JOYCE *move upstage to in front of the double doors as the others come in.* ARCHIBALD *goes to* CORNELIA'S *right and* RICHARD *and* BARBARA *remain left.*

Cornelia: Jubilate! Then there is hope of the villain being hanged at last.

Archibald: Well, it will go very hard with him. He will, at any rate, suffer a long term of imprisonment.

Cornelia: Imprisonment! Bah! Hang him at once! But how was this discovered?

Archibald: Otway Bethel has been in Norway since just after the murder of Mr Hallijohn but recently returned to this country. When he heard that an innocent man might be accused of the crime, he came forward and deposed that he saw Thorn, who we now know to be Levison, come from the cottage just after the fatal shot was fired.

Cornelia: But the scoundrel, Bethel, denied that at the time.

Archibald: Yes, but we now know that Levison bribed him with fifty pounds to keep silent on the matter. What is more, Joyce, your sister Afy has, this afternoon, confessed that Levison was with her in the cottage.

Barbara: I thank Heaven that my dear brother is restored to me at last.

Richard: Barbara, my dear sister. Mr Carlyle, sir, how can I thank you for all —

Archibald (*crossing to him*): Nonsense, you are my dear wife's brother. Come, we will go to your father and mother, Richard and give them the glad news.

All go off through the french window except JOYCE *and* WILSON.

Joyce: This is a happy day indeed for the Hares.

Wilson: I'll go and tell Cook — she'll be as excited as me when she hears the news. (*Exit right*).

JOYCE *moves over to stage left*.

Joyce: So my sister Afy has told the truth at last and all stain has been taken away from the good name of Richard Hare. It was that foul monster Levison who murdered my father and betrayed my dear lady.

The double doors open and ISABEL *staggers into the room and collapses against the framework of the door. She is not wearing her glasses.*

Joyce: Oh Madame Vine, what is it? (*Runs up to her*) Lady Isabel! Not dead — not dead!

Isabel: No. Oh would that I *were* dead. I recovered by a miracle and returned the shattered wreck you see me now — prematurely aged, crippled, broken-hearted. Oh that I had died and had been spared this agony. Oh my boy, my boy! (*Sobbing*) Oh my Willie!

Joyce: My lady what is it?

Isabel: He is dead — Willie is dead!

Joyce: Oh my lady. You ought not to have come here.

Isabel: I could not stay away longer from my children. Think you it has been no punishment to me being here, to see him, my husband once — the husband of another. It was killing me — and now to see my boy close his eyes on this world and me — I — I —

Joyce: Oh, come, my dear lady. I hear voices. Someone will come and you will be discovered.

Isabel: I care not now. Let them come. My life's sands are almost run. I feel faint — I — I — (*Coughs*).

Joyce (*leading her*): Come, my lady, lie down on the sofa. I will fetch a doctor. (*Puts her head on the sofa, head right end*).

Isabel: No — not a doctor, Joyce — it is too late. I fear I will not last this day out. Joyce — I should die happier if I might see Mr Carlyle.

Joyce: My lady! See him! See Mr Carlyle!

Isabel: What can it matter? I am already as one dead.

Joyce: It could not be, my lady. It must not be. It is as a thing impossible.

Isabel: Joyce, Joyce, let me see him!

Joyce: I will go and ask Miss Carlyle.

Isabel (*catching hold of* JOYCE *as she moves towards the door right*): No, Joyce — it is him that I wish to see — before I die.

Joyce: Quiet, my lady, do not distress yourself so. I will go and fetch Miss Carlyle. (*Exit right*).

Isabel (*raising herself up on one elbow*): Oh, Willie, Willie my child! He is dead, dead, dead. And he never knew me — never called me mother!

Enter CORNELIA *followed by* JOYCE *who remains by the door.* CORNELIA *comes and stands behind the sofa.*

Cornelia: What is this that Joyce has been telling me — mercy be good to us! How could you dare to come back here?

Isabel: My children — how could I stay away from them? Have pity Miss Carlyle! Don't reproach me. I am on my way to God, to answer for all my sins and sorrows.

Cornelia: I do not reproach you.

Isabel: I am so glad to go. I tried to take up my cross and bear it bravely but its weight has killed me.

Cornelia: Child, had I anything to do with sending you from East Lynne?

Isabel: You did not send me; you did not help to send me. I was not very happy with you, but that was not the cause of — of my going away. Forgive me, Miss Carlyle, forgive me.

Cornelia: Forgive *me*. I could have made your home happier, and I wish I had done so. I have wished it ever since you left.

Isabel: I want to see Archibald. I have prayed Joyce to bring him to me and she will not. Only for a minute. Just to hear him say that he forgives me. What can it matter, now that I am as one lost to this world? I should die easier.

Cornelia (*turning to* JOYCE): Joyce, go and request your master to come here.

Joyce: Oh, ma'am! Will it be well to tell him — well that he should see her?

Cornelia: Go and request your master to come at once. Are you mistress, Joyce, or am I?

    Exit JOYCE *right, crying.*

Cornelia: Now, my poor child, I will leave you. You shall see Archibald alone.

Isabel: God bless you, Cornelia — you are very kind — you have taken a heavy burden from off my soul.

    CORNELIA *bends over her and kisses her and exits right.*

Isabel: Now I shall see my dear husband once more — ask him to forgive me — and then shall I have done with life.

    Enter ARCHIBALD *right. He crosses behind the sofa and turns to face* ISABEL.

Archibald: I am grieved, Madame Vine to —

Isabel: Archibald!

Archibald: Isabel — is it you?

Isabel: I could not die without your forgiveness. Do not turn from me! Bear with me a little minute. Only say you forgive me, and I shall die in peace.

Archibald (*coming to the front of sofa and sitting on the left end*): Isabel! Are you — were you Madame Vine?

Isabel: Oh, forgive me, forgive me! I did not die. I recovered from that accident, but it changed me dreadfully; no one knew me, and I came here as Madame Vine. I could not stay away. Archibald forgive me! I could not stay away from you and my children. The longing for you was killing me. I never knew a moment's peace after the mad act I was guilty of in leaving you. Not an hour had departed when my repentance set in. See what it has done for me! My sin was great, but my punishment has been greater.

Archibald: Why did you go?

Isabel: Did you not know? I went out of love for you. I loved you dearly, and I grew suspicious of you. I thought you were false and deceitful to me; that your love was all given to another; and in my jealousy, I listened to the sore temptings of that bad man, who whispered to me of revenge. It was not so, was it?

Archibald: Can you ask it? I was never false to you in thought, in word, or in deed.

Isabel: I know it now, but I was mad. I never could have committed the act in anything but madness. Oh say that you will forgive and forget me!

Archibald: I cannot forget; I have already forgiven.

Isabel: Archibald, I am now on the threshold of the next world. Will you not bless me — will you not say a word of love to me before I pass it? Let what I am be blotted for the moment from your memory. Think of me as the innocent, timid child whom you made your wife. Only a word of love! My heart is breaking for it!

Archibald (*leaning over and kissing her forehead — in a whisper*): You nearly broke mine when you left me, Isabel. May God bless you and take you to His rest in Heaven.

72

Isabel: To His rest in Heaven. Keep a little corner in your heart for your poor lost Isabel.

Archibald: Yes — yes.

Isabel (*in pain*): Are you leaving me?

Archibald: You are growing faint, I perceive. I must call assistance.

Isabel: It is death, I think, not faintness. Oh, but it is hard to part! Farewell, farewell, my once dear husband. Farewell until eternity —

Archibald: Until eternity!

She dies in his arms. He raises his eyes to Heaven as

THE CURTAIN FALLS

THE END

PRODUCTION NOTES

Unlike any other version of this play, there is only one set. It is described at the beginning of Act One and is the conventional box-type set which was in vogue at the end of the last century. It should be realistic rather than representative and it should be over-furnished and over-dressed by modern standards.

CASTING

All other versions of this play include at least one small child. As the inclusion of children usually presents a number of difficulties, in this version they are referred to rather than seen. There should be no casting problems as the number of characters (5 women and 4 men) is within the scope of even the smallest group.

MUSIC

The other titles in this series — 'Sweeney Todd the Barber' and 'The Murder of Maria Marten' or 'The Red Barn' — both include a number of songs and background music. It was felt that songs would be an intrusion in this more realistic melodrama and so only one song is included (the music and lyrics appear in full on pages 76-79). This is not a interpolated song but an essential part of the story. The melody of this song is, however, very suitable for playing slowly as a background to some of the 'tragic' episodes of the play.

PROPERTIES

A full list of those referred to in the script appears on page 75.

LIGHTING

There are very few lighting cues — a full list appears on page 75.

COSTUME AND MAKE-UP

The period of the play is the mid 1850's but there is no reason why it should not be presented in any period from then until the turn of the century. The make-up of Isabel in the final act should be exaggerated — white hair, dark glasses, prematurely lined. The villain, Francis Levison should be dark-haired and wear a moustache (which he can twirl at appropriate moments). All the other characters are fairly straight forward but all should show some sign of the passing of ten years between the beginning and end of the play.

STYLE OF PERFORMANCE

This is a very different type of melodrama to 'Sweeney' and 'Maria'. In style it is much nearer to the more realistic plays of the Robertson and Pinero period. Although its sentimentality may seem absurd to modern audiences, it is far less crude than the earlier melodramas. The play should be acted very seriously with an edge of overplaying. This should result in far more laughter than a blatant burlesque. As in all melodramas, audience participation is most important and every effort should be made to encourage this.

LIGHTING PLOT

Evening — oil lamps on table left, piano and long table.
Lights fade to half at end of scene when Isabel and Archibald exit with
the lamp (from the long table.)
ACT I — SCENE 2
Daylight — (no cues).
ACT 2 — SCENE I
Daylight — (no cues).
ACT 2 — SCENE 2
Evening — oil lamps alight — (no cues).
ACT 3 — SCENE I
Evening — oil lamps lit — snow effect outside french window — (no
cues).
ACT 3 — SCENE 2
Daylight — (no cues).
ACT 3 — SCENE 3
Evening — summer — (no cues).

PROPERTY PLOT

Only those properties referred to in the script are listed here. Details of
the furniture and stage dressing are given at the beginning of Act One.

ACT I — SCENE I

Personal: ISABEL: Handkerchief
On Stage: Wine glasses
Decanter of wine
Jug of water
Tray

ACT I — SCENE 2

Personal: WILSON: Duster
BARBARA: Handkerchief
Locket
On Stage: Sheet music

ACT 2 — SCENE I

Personal: WILSON: Pan and brush
JOYCE: Flowers
On Stage: Vases

ACT 2 — SCENE 2

Personal: ARCHIBALD: Legal documents
On Stage: Pen, ink, paper and envelopes

ACT 3 — SCENE I

Personal: ARCHIBALD: Legal documents
Pen, ink and paper
Pocket watch
CORNELIA: Knitting box
Spectacles
On Stage: Decanter of brandy
Glasses and jug of water on tray

ACT 3 — SCENE 2

Personal: JOYCE: Letter
ISABEL: Dark glasses
On Stage: Sheet Music

THE YEARS THAT PASS AWAY

Music and lyrics by Brian J. Burton

Arranged by Sheila Corbett

Through the years that pass away
   I'll love you more and more
And your love for me, I pray,
   Will last for evermore.
Keep, within your heart my dear,
   A place where I may stay
That I may never need to fear
   The years that pass away.

As long as you are by my side
   I'll face whate'er may be
Until in Heaven we do abide
   For all eternity.

When those years have passed away
   And life is nearly o'er
Still your love for me, I pray
   Will be for evermore.
There, within your heart my dear,
   Forever I will stay
And never ever need to fear
   The years that pass away.
And never ever need to fear
   The years that pass away.